Hotel Secrets

*A Cautionary Tale of
Hope & Hospitality*

Harry Pope

Contents

Hotel Secrets
First published in 2019 by
AG Books
www.agbooks.co.uk

Digital edition converted and distributed by
Andrews UK Limited
www.andrewsuk.com

Prologue

Picture this scene... We are in the lounge of the Sheldon Hotel in Eastbourne, East Sussex. Present are the four joint owners– one local couple and a husband-and-wife from California in the USA. Their accountant is also in attendance, along with his assistant. Also seated is a senior representative from the commercial office of NatWest Bank. And a solicitor.

The local man and wife are the writer of this book, Harry, and his better half, Pam. They are in their 50s, with a very strong independent commercial background. He is almost bald, she is not. Somewhat comfortably proportioned, he has been self-employed for the past sixteen years, initially owning a South London executive car hire business, which they ran very successfully as a couple. They make an excellent team, have been married for well over thirty years, confide in each other, are comfortable with each other, and trust each other's judgment implicitly.

The Californian and his wife we shall call Mark and Deanna. *Not* their real names, because Harry is going to be revealing a lot, and doesn't particularly want to be sued... or worse. This comment will be explained as you read on.

They have been friends for six years, liking each other's company, but never really *close*. A mutual respect, however, has steadily grown. This is about to be shattered.

Mark is a businessman very close to the Pacific ocean. He has a factory that manufactures custom parts for vehicles that are out of production, particularly bumpers and exhausts. Ostensibly this is a very successful business, with twenty employees and no partners. Mark has never *had* a business partner. He is over six feet tall with a strong physique, and is *very* used to getting his own way with whatever he does. Quite ruthless, he loves to show power. Don't shake hands with Mark.

Deanna is lovely. She is from a family of airheads. Her mother and father invested in the factory, but are not *partners*, just *employees*. Mother has a lovely nature, just like her daughter, who likes to spend money. Deanna has accounts with *all* the shopping channels; going to the store isn't particularly important... but getting on that phone and having something delivered *is*. At home she has two pets: an indolent psychotic cat that bites the hand that feeds it (Nasty) and a miniature chihuahua dog (but which thinks it's a St. Bernard) that should be carried everywhere. Deanna is slim with the figure of a model in her 40s.

Mike, the account manager from NatWest, is one of the nicest bankers you could meet. He has a twinkle in his eye, can see beyond a balance sheet, and has been part of the business community for many years. He has a lot of contacts, and recommended the accountant. Mike is slim, he's wearing a conservative grey pin-striped suit, his thinning grey hair is cut short, and he comes across as one of the good guys in life. Which is true, because he is.

An accountant with a sense of humour? Yup, that is Steve; young for a junior partner in his 30s. He brings a wealth of experience to the meeting and is also respected in the local business community, which he has been a part of all his working years. Again, slim, he has discarded his jacket– still wearing his tie, though. A couple of children and their mother at home, Steve has the confidence of his position, knowing he is good at his job.

Alongside him is a very senior employee of the practice, a young man who will go places because he is driven by ambition. Shrewd, gives good advice when asked, otherwise he just listens. Matt is one of those driven to succeed in what profession he chose, it is just coincidental that accountancy is what he is doing; it could be anything and he would be good at it.

There are three top legal practices in Eastbourne. One man present is senior partner with number three. Again, he has a lot of local knowledge; he's respected, influential. Tubby, short and bald... but don't let appearances deceive. He's a very shrewd man. Harry doesn't want to describe him *too* well, as this man is still actively involved in the Eastbourne business community, and despite the fact that they haven't met for many years, it could prove embarrassing for both as the events of this sorry tale evolve.

The door to the hotel lounge is closed, and this is the very first gathering of all of them, despite the fact that the hotel has been owned by the partnership for three months already. That is because Mark and Deanna have not been able to travel over since before Christmas due to commitments in California, so all present are intrigued to discuss the first three months.

'So, you have all seen the figures for the first three months,' said Harry. 'Bearing in mind they have been February March and April, the leanest time of the hotel year, I think I can be conservatively pleased. They are certainly an improvement on those provided to us by the previous owners– up by 20%, but bear in mind that they were somewhat underplayed for accountancy reasons.'

Steve the accountant: 'I think that these figures cause no concern, they have met what Harry said before the hotel was purchased; so far he has been proven right.'

Mike the banker: 'I agree. He didn't try to forecast spectacular figures, and we haven't got those. But they do show movement in the right direction.'

Mark the Californian partner: 'I am glad we are all agreed, because I have to share something with you that none of you are aware of. That is, due to my debt situation in California, I need to have £6,000 transferred across every month to cover my outlay.'

The room went very quiet.

Steve said 'but that *just can't happen.*'

Mark replied 'It *MUST* happen. I have debts that have to be covered.'

Steve: 'What debts?'

Mark: 'Credit cards.'

Harry: 'What credit cards?'

Mark: 'You didn't realise, but when I was raising my share, I was short, so had to borrow on my credit cards.'

Harry: 'How much did you have to borrow?'

Mark: '£100,000'.

Steve: 'A new business just can't sustain that level of debt. You will never retrieve what you put in. On that basis, my advice would be to sell the hotel immediately and cut your losses.'

Harry knew that from that moment on, his partnership in the Sheldon Hotel, Eastbourne, was doomed.

...

And he was right.

Hotel Secrets

Chapter One: How It Started

We had lived in Cheam on the South London and north Surrey borders for the majority of our lives. Married in 1973, I had been involved in the funeral profession for many years, almost the start of our marriage, and in 1990 we had started our own business. This was called Cheam Limousines.

January 1990 I bought my first commercial vehicle, which was a basic model Daimler DS420 limousine. For those unaware, this had no air conditioning, a fridge in winter and an oven in summer, made by Daimler/Jaguar as a specialist limousine. By four years we had added a Mercedes 500 S Class in white; another couple of years and we had expanded sufficiently to have five cars and two full time drivers as well as me and a team of part-time drivers. That was when the first major contract arrived.

Cheam Limousines had a nucleus of about a dozen travel agents in America sending their clients over to us for sight-seeing and airport transfers, and one of them mentioned that a major Californian travel company were expanding their European business. Based in Athens, operating there and Italy, they were expanding into Paris and London. After three fraught months of submitting plans to them, they decided on little Cheam Limousines in the UK, with five cars, and in Paris the largest chauffeur company with 95 vehicles. That was a real boost to us, one we were to capitalise on.

This was a superb time for us, the middle to late 1990s, plenty of money earned, good lifestyle, excellent friends, we were in our early 50s, good prospects, business expanding, and then we met Mark and Deanna.

They were clients from California, using the travel company for their journeys, real Anglophiles having been to the UK many times. They usually stayed at the Ritz Hotel in London, sometimes at the Savoy, and this fateful day I was their chauffeur for the journey between Gatwick and London. Cheam is about midway, me being me I suggested they could break their journey for a comfort stop. Mostly when this was offered the clients turned it down, but I suppose this pair wanted to see a local English family. I rang Pam, warned her we were stopping, and they stayed for dinner, sharing the family sausages and mash.

I walked them into Cheam village to the butchers, Mark and Deanna were impressed we still had a local family run shop selling meat, they chose the bangers, and after the early meal dropped them off back at their London hotel. I loved to share our environment with my guests, seeing it as a welcome to the UK. There was a standard patter as they were driven through the English countryside.

'Over on your left you can see something you are not used to at home. It's coloured green, and is called grass.'

Gasp of amazement.

'Standing on that new phenomena is something tall, brown, and also has a different colour green attached. That is called a tree, and the green are ..leaves.'

Good gags, all part of the Cheam Limousines experience.

I thought no more of the couple until it was time to return to Gatwick. Details were exchanged, I looked his business up on the internet, which looked impressive.

Over the next five years they returned three times, each time I was their driver, and they were really interested when I told them that in 2003 Pam and I were selling up, moving to the south coast, to buy an eight bedroom B&B in a resort called Eastbourne. They had never heard of it, so looked it up to discover it was mid-way between Brighton and Hastings, population about 100,000, very genteel, with a pier and four theatres.

The reason for the move was quite simple – I was killing myself running the business. Five stones overweight, drinking too much, eating the wrong food when out on the road, I was fainting, nose bleeds, high blood pressure, all the usual symptoms. So the business was sold to one of our drivers for a reasonable figure, the family home was sold, and we came to live by the seaside.

The move occurred in June 2003, a Summer with the least amount of rain for many years. There were only six days that Summer when rain fell, which was to be a blessing for us, as the mid-terrace 1892 house required much work doing to it.

***

The details can be boring, not quite relevant to this tale, but in the space of less than three months we changed it from an eight bedroom house with one room en suite to a six bedroom one with all rooms complete with facilities. The Mercedes E class saloon as well as Pam's Hyundai Accent saloon car came to the seaside with us, and Harry drove Pam's little car to the tip over one hundred times. The superfluous Mercedes was soon sold.

Two neighbours were engaged as the builders and joint project managers, at a quite considerable fee on reflection, we were the labourers to cut down on expenses. There is a nationwide builders merchants' called Wickes with a local branch, and I became such a regular, and also a nuisance with constant demands, that on one occasion I entered the store as one of the female staff was on the public address system. Her eyes followed me as I walked past her, she was incapable of speech, mute until I was gone, still with microphone in her hands.

Why? Well, just for example, Colin would send me there to get some plumbing. He was always specific, because he knew that I am an impractical man, with hands only there to use a computer, or feed my face, certainly not to hold a saw, or a hammer, or a screwdriver, definitely not a paintbrush. Colin knew he had to write down specifically what was required, as I had a habit of returning with the incorrect item, albeit only marginally wrong, but you could be sure that it would not fit in the designated hole. Hence the nervousness of the Wickes staff, dreading my entrance as they would be required to issue a refund, and then walk with me to the correct shelf, which frequently was lacking the exact required item.

That was my introduction to the Eastbourne hotel business.

We immediately became members of the local Hotel Association, quite active socially, and it was strange to sit with over a dozen other men over a delicious meal with red wine discussing the merits of which store sold the best sausages for guests at breakfast. Bizarre, really.

We opened our doors to guests in late September, had missed the whole of the money earning Summer season, so were ready to welcome the non-existent Winter guests. The house had previously been run on an economy basis mainly for students, so we had to create a new market from nothing, at the wrong end of the season. Lousy timing, but it wasn't our fault, as we had been trying to move in for a long time, with solicitors as usual holding up procedures.

One idea I had that first winter was to prove quite successful. I purchased some bottles of inexpensive wine during a shopping visit to France, and then went into all thirty three Eastbourne estate agents, with a bottle for each one and some business cards and brochures. The impact of a free bottle of wine was great, and the guest house had quite a few people stay with us who were recommended in this way.

We had kept in touch with our Californian friends, who were to come and stay with us on two occasions as paying guests. The foursome socialised, they came to the Hotel Association's annual black tie dinner, they came to the group events, fitting in very well. Mark and Deanna just loved the feel of the area, as it is in a wide bay, with Beachy Head cliffs to the west, and Hastings to the east. It has the South Downs five miles behind, so the atmosphere is conducive to a pleasant stay. Okay, there's some wind, but it is a very easy climate to live in, which coming from California they were to appreciate.

We had owned the B&B for just under three years, gaining more success each season, when I had a phone call from Mark quite out of the blue. One evening he rang and asked if we would like to go into business with him and his wife to buy a larger hotel. In Eastbourne. Budget to be discussed later, this was just a preliminary call.

What to do, risk everything, or stay where you were?

Staying where we were was just an option, as we had a sizeable mortgage, and would be paying it off a long way in the future. By this time we were just short of 60, not fancying the prospect of working until we were in our mid 70s before being able to retire. There's not much glamour, being a B&B owner, you get up early to start preparing the breakfasts, and there's not a lot of pleasure cleaning a shower, let alone head stuck down a toilet. Two of the toilets had macerators, those strange contraptions that munch the effluent so it will go through a smaller waste pipe. On one memorable occasion some idiot guest blocked it with something too big, despite a large notice on the wall, and Harry had to clear. Unfortunately, the neighbour who came to assist thought he knew everything, turning on the power while it was disconnected, effluent covering walls, ceilings, floor, and me. I had to strip to my underpants in the back garden and wash off everything under a hose with cold water. It was such a hot April day that my mouth was really dry, so licked my lips. Before realising how badly I was covered. Yuck.

Did I embrace the prospect of performing this into my dotage?

However, buying a larger hotel in partnership with people we had only met previously on half a dozen occasions, albeit a week at a time, was not a decision to be taken lightly. Mark was very persuasive, holding out the future of hotel ownership, maybe a group of half a dozen similarly sized establishments, quality guests, not getting hands dirty, financial security for the rest of our lives.

We went for it.

***

'So Mark, what budget do we have? Do we have a million? Two million? I really don't know what to look at, what our price range is.'

'Harry, look at it this way, we will know when we see the right hotel. It might take a few weeks, it might take a few months, but we will know when the right one comes along. Just keep on looking, then let me know.'

It was obvious to us that Mark and Deanna flew first class everywhere, they stayed first class, they used the travel company Cheam Limousines worked for and their client list was pretty wealthy, so I was aware that Pam and I were entering into a business plan with someone of substance. Just to probe, we suggested he had a look at one on the market for £2.4 million.

'That's okay Harry, have a look and let me know.'

Mark didn't even blanch, which was certainly out of the prospective range. We knew that after we had paid off our B&B mortgage and financial commitments we would be left with about £50k, so the main financial burden was going to fall on Mark's shoulders. There wasn't the slightest doubt about his probity.

Mark and Deanna's business was mail order all over the USA, and had a good turnover and healthy customer base. He had been going for over twenty years, advertised in all the speciality magazines, and was the leader in his market. Just to give you an example of the home trappings, London Transport had a policy of selling off a large number of Route master double decker buses. The phone conversation with Harry went like this:

'Harry, can you have a look at seeing how much it would cost to transport a London transport bus back to California. How long it would take, The practicalities, that kind of thing.'

He bought one. Paid for it to be shipped over to California, which cost over £5,000 alone, then restored it to a high degree. This was all done on a whim by an ostensibly wealthy American.

They owned a 40ft mobile home, touring round the US as much as business commitments permitted, but in reality it was parked up for years at a time, as they tended to come to the UK for holidays. Another expensive toy.

What should have concerned me was a phone call I received from Mark when we were at the looking at hotels stage. As Mark's father in law worked with him, he had received an e-mail from a USA based lottery company stating he had won over $1m. Mark rang me for my opinion, if his father in law should contact them to claim the prize. Mark was asked one simple question.

'Does your father in law play the lottery?'

'No.'

'Then how could he possibly have won anything then.'

End of conversation, but there should have been alarm bells for obvious reasons.

As it happened, Pam didn't like the £2.4m seafront hotel, it was a lovely building, but the owner was an idiot who hadn't spent anything on it. There were 46 bedrooms, superb location, but it was obvious all rooms were very tired and another million would have been necessary to get it up to standard. We looked elsewhere. As it transpires, this particular hotel did ultimately change hands to an upmarket consortium, has had a lot of money spent and invested, but despite its prestigious prime location has proved to be a major white elephant. Just goes to show that some properties just can't make money.

The agent told us about a reasonably sized hotel adjacent to the seafront. It had been derelict for at least six years. We were showed around with lots of health warnings. In through the main door visitors were confronted by a reception desk. Behind the desk there were no floorboards, and you could see into the depths of the basement. Walking around, it was a wonder to all that it had only been six years, the last paying guests being a coach party with lowered standards. The room rate was considerably cheaper as well.

We all went all round this hotel very carefully, ignoring the missing floor sections, it had a lot of potential. It would have been a necessity to clean the place up as well, removing the large dead rats from the basement (yes, really), but it was a lovely elegant façade with a decent back garden/terrace for secluded exclusive guest use. The cost was around half a million pounds, but a buyer had to look at spending twice that amount just to get it up to standard, and the same again to make it a really classy hotel to attract the right kind of guest that Mark was interested in.

Any prospective purchaser was also looking at a year-long building project, with the prospect of longer if the builders were errant. The budget would have had to be flexible, because you never knew what you were going to find requiring fixing in an 1890 building such as this. Not for the faint hearted expecting fast returns on capital investment.

That autumn Mark and Deanna came to our guest house to stay with us for a week. They never offered to pay for their accommodation, which was a first. The couple didn't do too much, just enjoyed staying in the premier bedroom, walking along the seafront, eating in the best local pub, *The Marine*. After a few days of this idyllic stay, I received a phone call from another hotelier.

'Harry, I know that Mark and Deanna are with you at present. Are you still looking at properties?'

'Yup, what do you have in mind?'

'Well, I know that David and Louise are thinking of selling the Sheldon, but haven't done anything about it. They can't make up their minds, she wants to go to Spain for a year or so, he wants to keep the hotel. Any sale would have to be discreet, there would be agents involved, but I just wonder if you are interested.'

'Certainly would be, what would be the price range?'

'Just shy of a million.'

'That could be very interesting. What would we do next?'

'Let me have a word with David, sound him out. But don't do anything yet, that is important, it's David we have to convince here.'

After coming off the phone, I turned to Pam, Mark and Deanna. 'That was a pal of mine, he has heard that the Sheldon COULD be up for sale, but we have to approach this very carefully.'

'Where is it?'

I told them.

Despite warnings to be discreet, that was it, he had the bit between his teeth, and he was off for a walk to have a look, even though he was told to go nowhere near the place.

Of course, Mark had to go alone, because I didn't want the seller to appreciate the enthusiasm my partner had for the project. He was simply desperate to buy somewhere, anywhere would do, as long as it was a project he could work with as soon as possible.

He got back, having talked to the owner's son, who had given him a look round. Before anyone knew it, an offer of £900,000 was made, no consultation with his potential business partners, the bid of course was rejected. The price was £975,000, and the owner wasn't prepared to budge, no surprise really, because he knew a sucker when he saw one.

As a builder, he had bought the hotel as a project, somewhat run down, so converted all the downstairs into four very large apartment rooms. They were stunning, a credit to his skills, just a shame that the other twenty four rooms didn't match.

Chapter Two: The Building

There were eight single bedrooms, two triples, the rest either with twin or double beds. All 28 bedrooms over the three floors and basement had their own bathrooms, with two more rooms on the ground floor behind the bar and restaurant, a single and double.

Looking at the outside of the Sheldon, there were two sets of stairs, which was because when originally built in the 1890s it was two semi-detached houses, or duplex as described in the USA. Two different families originally lived there, the building was only converted in the 1950s to one hotel. There was a gap on the left between the boundary wall and the hotel itself, likewise on the right. The left area had been utilised with a fence, behind which was a couple of sheds, which we used for storing goods in freezers.

At the top of the steps was a small area with a metal framed bench seat, often used in warm weather. At the bottom of the steps were two outside cupboards, one for storage including a complicated electricity board, the other with a door, behind which was the lift mechanism. This door was locked. The electricity cupboard also had a door, because hidden in the corner were thirty six metal banisters from the original building in 1890s, removed when the house was made into one hotel. They hadn't been touched for many years, no rust, just cobwebs. These were to be forgotten for a long time.

On the right side of the hotel, instead of a fence, an addition to the hotel had been connected, two rooms, one a double, the other a single. They had a flat roof, never a damp problem as it had been erected properly, but they were pretty basic rooms with en suite, nothing special.

However, under previous ownership the whole of the basement had been used as accommodation for the building's owner and family and servants. The reason why I previously mentioned that the man we bought the Sheldon from was a builder, was because he was responsible for the conversion of the basement into four ostensibly really lovely apartment rooms.

Each room was very big, with sumptuous lounge furniture, faux marble bathrooms, and a separate entrance from the hall into the secluded car park, which had room at the back for twenty considerately parked vehicles. The car park was Tarmaced, but had a drain in the middle that required frequent unblocking when weather inclement. On one memorable occasion I forgot to clear it for a few weeks, when it rained really heavily I had to wade out into the middle, with a garden fork, raise the cover, then put my hand down in the cold dirty water and free the leaves. Couldn't find a staff member to volunteer so it had to be me. Owner's perks of the job.

Inside the front door was an inner door with top half glass, then the reception area. On the left was the ladies loo, next door the gents, and Harry and Pam have never forgotten hearing the shriek coming from one lady guest when sitting quietly with the window open when drowned by a gush of water. The idiot window cleaner had used his hose unwisely.

Next to the loos was the lift, sufficiently large for three people plus luggage, but whatever you do, don't overload. This never happened during our ownership, we were respectful of the lift mechanism.

Facing you as you walked in was the reception desk.

This was quite high, with low desk behind, so you had to peer up at anyone taller than Dolly Parton. There was a diary system, everything entered by hand, nothing to back-up so if that got lost or stolen for any reason then we would have been scuppered. Behind the receptionist's head was a hatch, which opened into the kitchen for ease of conversation. Or shout at them if they had been recalcitrant.

The front rooms of the hotel consisted of lounge and bar. The lounge had outdated furniture, a writing desk, settees, wing backed chairs that should belong in a hotel lobby, and blue fitted carpet with rugs covering immovable stains. It is quite obvious that staff occasionally went down the back of the chairs to find lost property after the guest had departed, we do hope so because that meant they were cleaning properly. Some hopes of that.

The bar was a large-ish room, bench seat window, metal lockable bars for the counter that would be secured in place against the wall, with behind the bar sufficiently large for one person no wider than a supermodel like Naomi Campbell. Not that she ever came to the Sheldon. More trouble than she would have been worth. Must stop fantasising and writing about beautiful women and return to the narrative.

There was a large TV on a high wall bracket, which had been previously connected to one of those systems that operated on wiring for the picture signal. The junction box was still on the window sill, it would have been quite a thing to remove, so as it wasn't doing any harm it remained in situ for the whole of our ownership, and is likely still there years later.

Alongside the back wall of the bar was a door into a hall, with storage cupboards, and the two additional rooms, one single one double, already mentioned. Back of the hall was a door to the dining room, which was an ostensibly beautiful feature of the hotel. The trouble was, both rooms of the dining area had original sash windows, listed, but rotting and draughty. Very high ceilings which went with a building of that venerable age, end of the dining room a swing door into the kitchen, said door had glass panel for obvious reason.

The kitchen was remarkably well appointed, quite modern, certainly fit for purpose, with frequent health inspections passing every time without complication. Easy to clean and maintain.

Metal steps down to the ground level, with the two sheds containing freezers. The car park had all the parking spaces clearly marked, a couple of decent large trees that didn't get in the way at all. There was also a metal emergency staircase from the car park that went into the building on the first floor, installed when the Sheldon was converted.

Typically in a building of that age, the stairs to the first floor were wide and long. The carpet was only in the middle, it would require replacing at some stage but they could cope with it for the present. It was reasonably dark, without any natural light, as all the windows were in the guest bedrooms. Central landing with lots of rooms off either side, likewise the second floor. The lift went to the first and second floors, and the Sheldon also had four top floor rooms, two on either side of the building. These had originally been servant's quarters when the building was constructed.

The stairs were quite narrow to access these rooms, so were let out last. No discount of course, but guests were always warned in advance. These four rooms were really very pleasant ones, ceilings coming down at an angle so bed positioning was carefully planned. TV signal was fine, the views were superb, some guests requested these rooms, but not often.

Chapter Three: Planning and Staffing

Planning meant discussing the financial set-up with the solicitor, accountant and bank. Bank was first, because without the finance in place nothing else would work. We were already banking with one of the big four banks with the B&B, so it was logical to use them for the hotel. Eastbourne might have a population of over 100,000, but it's like a village, with a business community scratching each others' backs. The bank recommended an accountant.

David is a lovely man, but he won't be embarrassed by identifying in this story, as this wasn't the best period in his professional life. His advice was spot-on for the most part, and he held hands when required. He recommended the solicitor, who was a real bummer. I met him a long time after, but he always swore he gave us some advice that we failed to act upon. Pam is pretty astute, pays attention just as much as I do if not more, and we are both of the opinion that we were never given the advice to create a partnership agreement. A lot would have transpired in a different way if it had. All water under the bridge, but a lot of money was paid for legal advice that turned out to be rubbish.

If we had entered the partnership advice as he said and failed to act on it, then his duty was to remind us again and suggest during further detailed business discussions that we had failed to act on his advice. He says he only told us once, we know he didn't. It all comes down to, he said/we didn't listen.

The way it was set up doesn't matter now, suffice to say all were very happy to enter the agreement and sign the documents presented in front of them by the respected solicitor.

Staffing could have been a problem, but as it turned out we landed on our feet. We had been active line dancers, and one of the ladies was a particularly good friend. She was a single lady, working in a senior capacity for quite a few years for a national company with a local office, but wanted a change in her life. This story will hide her identity by referring to her by the nickname we were to ultimately give her. Moaner.

We discussed what would be a reasonable salary, and she informed us that she required £25,000 per annum to be our general manager. A grand title for a role that we were to fulfil ourselves, we would have done a lot better by paying two thirds to someone else far more experienced and competent, but we were on a learning curve. The hotel had an annual turnover of £280,000, so we thought the establishment could afford this for reliable and honest assistance. Mark and Deanna had been introduced to Moaner on a previous visit, they were very satisfied with the choice, recognising that help would be needed.

Kitchen staff were also necessary. We were regulars in a lovely privately run Eastbourne hotel, the chef was pretty good but unrecognised by the majority of the customers, as well as management. Their opinion was staff were expendable, especially those originating in Poland, which to an extent was true. If ever any staff were needed, all they had to do was mention it on the Polish grapevine and they were inundated with more than suitable applicants. A private word was had with Anya, the cook, who had been a teacher back home. Her partner was Artur, who had been a graphic designer, was a supremely talented photographer, more than capable of being Anya's kitchen porter – a glorified washer upper and menial food preparer. He had never done it before, but as a means to earning some money had no problems. Unfortunately his demeanour was often sad, as he hated what he was doing, and he was to be given a nickname as well. Ee-aw, the donkey. We never knew what his mood would be when he reported for work each morning. However, when he covered for Anya, what he prepared was superb.

A housekeeper was also required, word was put about, and Sheila (not her real name, but sufficiently close) applied. She was a very pretty lady in her mid twenties, who knew if she was any good at cleaning, but she came recommended, which was sufficient for us. We had to have someone, after all.

She was to be the only initial housekeeper, our plan was to engage someone extra as and when required. Moaner and Pam covered Anya's day off, we also took on Baby Artur, another Pole who was fabulous. We only called him 'baby' because he was younger and smaller than the other Artur. Happy to be adaptable, he could cover the bar, night porter, waiting at table, kitchen assistant, the only thing he didn't do was clean the rooms. He was also something of a handyman, so if maintenance was required, then we got him to do it.

Mark and Deanna came over early December, plans were in place, all we needed was for the legalities to be completed. The owners wanted to sell, we wanted to buy, but the lawyers decided to take three weeks off for the Christmas and New Year break. It's not until you experience these frustrations that you fully appreciate the frailties of the system. Each legal office blames the other. One wants to ask extra questions, the other then has to inform their client. The information goes back and forth, inventories have to be completed, which bear no relation to what is handed over. How many chairs in the lounge. How many single beds. What rooms have televisions. They all do of course, what a dumb question, it's not us doing the asking, but the information still has to be shared, it's all part of the process of them justifying their money. I had told my solicitor that part of our agreement was he was doing all of this for a fixed fee, so he would also act for us in the sale of the B&B. However long he took, there would be no extra coming across, so if I hadn't tied him to this then who knows how long it would have taken.

January was spent in a long month of frustration, then we moved in the first Friday of February.

***

We woke early, excited, on an early February morning. We were going to buy The Sheldon Hotel in Eastbourne. Today. A 28 bedroom hotel, own car park, detached, prestige establishment, maybe in need of some TLC, but still pretty good. And it was going to be ours. Well, not strictly ours, half would be owned by our business partner and his wife, but the majority would be owned by NatWest Bank. But one day it would all be ours.

Before we could take possession, with the assistance of those lovely people who would be lending us the money, there was something mundane for me to do. Pass an exam.

If you want to sell alcohol to the public in the UK, you have to have a licence. To obtain this piece of paper, you have to place forty correct ticks onto an idiot proof sheet of paper. There are four potential answers to each of the forty questions, each option is for simpletons to get wrong, and the pass requirement is thirty five correct. You have to prove your competence to know the law to serve alcohol in any questionable situations, such as the four options to one question. The question is this...

A five year old child comes up to your bar and asks for a whisky. Do you:

  1. Ask for his ID

  2. Refuse to serve him

  3. Look for his parents

  4. Ask him if he wants water and ice with it

Okay, I may have exaggerated somewhat, but you get the picture. Anyone with less than a full score sheet doesn't deserve to be in the business in the first place. But if I didn't pass, then I would not be allowed to open the bar that night, and have to wait another month before re-sitting. No pressure then.

I sat the exam at 9am, exiting at 9:45am. Relieved, I drove back to where I was living, then waited for the phone call to say we could move in. Within ten minutes, no anxious wait, it was ours.

The man who sold to us was something of a taciturn man, stout of stature, building background, tall, with a very attractive wife with a long pedigree of local family hotel ownership. He wasn't too keen on me, because when negotiating everything, I had insisted that a clause was inserted whereby they couldn't own a hotel within two years and ten miles of our present location. This didn't suit his business plans, but I was aware of history.

We were given the half hour tour, handed over the keys, and that was it.

Let me try to recount some of the conversation as Pam and I followed him around.

'This is the electrical cupboard for the left side of the building, lower floors. It's an outside cupboard, alongside the lift, you can see that the power supply is on. If there is an interruption, it cuts out. The power, that is. You come to this cupboard, flip this trip switch up, and bingo, there's light again. The lift has a maintenance contract with Thyssen Krupp, pay the bills and they'll never have to come out.'

'Upstairs, on the first floor landing, is another cupboard. This also has a board with switches. All the lights go out on two floors on this side of the building, stick your head in this cupboard, flip the switch.'

'On the right side, whatever you do, don't let the electricity supply be interrupted. That's because, despite the fact that there's a switch board, you'll never get into it. Go on, open this door. See it there. It's on the far wall. Now try and get inside the cupboard. You can't, can you? I certainly can't, and I'm a lot bigger than you. But there's a broom handle just here. Grab hold of it, that's right, point it at the far wall. No, don't touch the wires, despite the handle being made of wood, you might, just might, make it go bang. Better call in someone to fix it. But only as long as they are small, like a young woman. A child would be better.'

'Now we are on the top floor landing. Here's the last power cupboard. That's right, you'll need a torch, so make sure you always have one handy. Never know when you'll need one.'

'Here's the keys, enjoy owning The Sheldon. By the way, you've got fourteen dinners for tonight, and we haven't taken their orders.'

'Oh yes, and when it rains really heavy, make sure that the basement doors are closed nice and tight, 'cause the rain gets in.'

Many years later Pam and I were on a cruise. We were walking through the bar on the way to dinner on the first night and heard this man and his wife talking loudly over drinks with their company. What a coincidence. We had maintained the infrequent acquaintance over the years, saying hello when meeting socially in Eastbourne, so after the initial hotel purchase were still sufficiently friendly to have the occasional chat.

So that was it. 10:30am Friday in February, and we were in possession. Rooms to check, dinners to prepare, and a party to organise.

Chapter Four: The First Three Months

I was speaking to Mark on a daily basis, reporting on business, figures, prospects, also e-mailing, so he and Deanna were completely aware of what was occurring. Inevitably, it was a learning curve for all of us, Pam and I less so, as we were the ones with experience and also in charge.

That first day went by in a blur. We cooked dinner for the guests, as the business we had bought was mainly people staying for bed breakfast and evening meal, or half board as is more commonly referred to. Nothing spectacular here, just plain English food matching the clientele. Mark wanted to up the guest quality. We were unrated, mainly because of the fact that we didn't really fall into any particular category.

We called ourselves a hotel, which of course we were, but the main rating company, the motoring organisation the AA, had one to five-star ratings for different accommodations. For example, our B&B, was rated three-star guest accommodation. You could have a pub with rooms, or a farmhouse, or variations on that theme, so I suggested that we went for guest accommodation, with the standards not so stringent as those for a hotel. Of course, that meant we couldn't call ourselves a hotel any more, but that didn't matter.

I contacted the AA, and requested a pre-rating visit, so we would know what we had to do to get a rating. Mark was particularly dim here, being obsessed with a five-star rating but not appreciating what that entailed. A five-star hotel is what he and Deanna were used to, such as The Ritz, or Savoy in London, or the Grand in Eastbourne. They had to provide a spa, beauty treatment, swimming pool, 24-hour room service, none of which we could possibly provide. However, we could be guest accommodation four star. The rooms just weren't sufficiently luxurious to get any more, and that would be pushing it. The AA man came for a fee of £250 for half a day, had a very good look round, and said we would just about manage a two-star rating guest accommodation without doing anything else.

Mark was devastated when I told him this, demanding a different assessor, it was with difficulty that I managed to get through to him that wasn't going to happen. If we wanted a higher grade, we would have to spend money, and that was a commodity in short supply.

He loved to come up with grand ideas. The front garden was split, with two very large fir trees so tall they were blocking light to public rooms on the ground floor, almost reaching the guest rooms on the first. I had to apply for Council planning permission to remove these two trees, while waiting Mark rang me one day. The conversation went something like this.

'Harry, you know those two trees in the front garden, what do you want to do when they are removed?'

'I would like to have the area landscaped, bring in a local gardener, make the whole area really attractive.'

'How close is Eastbourne to Nottingham?'

'Why?'

'Because I have been online and discovered a Nottingham factory that makes garden fountains at a very reasonable figure.'

'What do you regard as reasonable?'

'Ten thousand.'

'Pounds or dollars?'

'Pounds.'

I had to think very fast here. I knew I was dealing with a child-like mentality that loved to spend big, while at the same time had to mollify my business partner. A simply said explanation was required.

'Okay, let's return to profitable figures. You know that before paying bank fees etc., we are working on roughly one third profit margin. So that means if we spend, say, £10,000 on an advertising campaign, we would have to increase our turnover by £30,000 just to stand still. So spend £10,000 to gain an extra £30,000 worth of business. Yes?'

Mark replied 'Yes.'

I then said, 'So do you think that a £10,000 fountain will generate an extra £30,000 worth of business? Do you think that all those extra hundreds of guests will decide to stay with us *just because* we have a lovely fountain in our front garden? A fountain that will require maintenance, staffing, and possibly be subject to vandalism? I know what my opinion is here Mark; I am intrigued to hear what yours is as well.'

'Okay Harry, you've made your point. We can't afford the fountain. But one day... maybe we will.'

***

Our daily routine was having a poor effect on my waistline. There was a three week period between when we bought the hotel and still owned the B&B, so Pam and Moaner were preparing and serving breakfasts at the hotel while I looked after our other guests. I am not a bad cook, can easily cope with serving six breakfasts, then servicing the rooms, ready for the next occupants. However, we realised that as we needed to maximise the hotel income, and Pam's elderly Aunty Joan was living with us, it would be impractical to live at the hotel.

Aunty was about ninety by this stage, quite active, but we didn't really want to share our living accommodation with the public. We rented a flat. This was the best possible move for us, so we would walk ten minutes to the hotel every morning. Quite often I would arrive first with the morning papers, and ensure that all was ready in kitchen and dining room. Moaner would arrive when she felt like it, manning the reception desk as I assisted the waiting staff. Serving breakfast was a real pleasure to me, interacting with the sometimes sharp witted guests. My favourite was to hover over them as they were finishing their cereal, saying in a loud Basil Fawlty voice 'come on, come on, your cooked breakfast is in the kitchen getting cold. Eat faster, eat faster.'

I managed to get away with this all the time, clearing away plates, serving the toast tea and coffee, washing up in the kitchen, overseeing what was occurring. When peace and calm were restored, empty restaurant, we would then sit down and have ours, that would be me, Pam and Moaner. We would be frequently interrupted by guests at the reception desk, asking futile obvious questions such as

- 'How long will it take us to walk into town?'
- 'Where are the shops?'
- 'What time is dinner?'

The answers are in the following order:

- 'Stand on the top step of the hotel, look into the distance, and you can see the town centre.'
- 'Same answer as in question one.'
- 'Have you given in your choice of evening dinner menu? Of course you have, and at the top, above the choices, it tells you munching times.'

Okay, I may not have been quite so acerbic, but it was pretty tempting to be. This is because my breakfast had been interrupted. That meal would consist of sausages that had been cooked for two hours and surplus to guest requirements, bacon that was shrivelled at the edges, tough because it had been cooked for so long, maybe some almost dried baked beans, fried eggs that had congealed, and a fresh pot of coffee. No wonder my waistline was suffering.

Up and down, up and down, from table to reception desk, food getting colder, the other two just chatting away as they enjoyed the breakfast break. Then I would disappear into my basement office and read the paper. Let them get on with it now.

***

Our housekeeper was a lovely lady, working hard on her own, no supervision, as we thought she was doing a good job, no feedback but all seemed to be well. She liked to finish as soon as she could, for reasons unknown at the time, but all was revealed when Mr and Mrs. Price came to stay.

They were repeat guests of many years standing, staying with a succession of owners, always had room three, booked a few weeks in advance, we had never met them previously, so it was a pleasure to welcome them as new proprietors. I had a policy of always carrying the luggage to the room, but never once received a gratuity. It was a good welcome for the guests, seeing the guvnor taking the baggage, they were no different. But half an hour later, Mr. Price was back downstairs.

Looking at me chatting to Pam and Moaner, he said 'Mr. Pope, would you kindly come upstairs with me to see Mrs. Price. There is a problem with the room.'

Pam and Moaner looked at each other, grateful it was me going to deal with a problem. That seemed to be more of my role these days, trouble shooting, so I wasn't particularly bothered. I should have been.

Room three was one of our better rooms, quite large, on the first floor, with lovely views. He took me into the bathroom, running his index finger over the top of the edge of the mirror. Dust.

'Would you please have a look in the shower, specifically the plug hole, and tell me what you see.'

I bent over in the shower.

'Human hair.'

'That's correct. Now would you care to lift the bedclothes, move the bed a few inches, and tell me what you see underneath.'

Not just dust motes, but bloody big balls you could have played tennis with. The mice must have been rolling them around for fun.

'Now Mr. Pope, we are reasonable people, we like staying at The Sheldon, we are not seeking a monetary reduction, we just want to stay somewhere that has the same standards we employ at home. I don't consider that unreasonable, do you?'

'No Mr. Price. One of our executive rooms on the lower ground floor is available, we normally charge a premium, but would you care to occupy there for your visit at no extra charge.'

'That would be very acceptable.'

I facilitated the move, then had a chat with Moaner.

'Let's get something really clear. That was one of the most difficult conversations in my life, and it's all because you didn't do your job properly. We pay you a considerable sum to be general manager, and part of that role is to supervise the staff. One of those staff is our housekeeper, and she obviously hasn't performed properly. What have you got to say.'

'It's not my fault if she hasn't done her job properly. You took her on. You should have checked her work, not me.'

Wrong thing to say to me, especially as she is on such an excellent screw, and I am on £2.80 an hour.

'Let's get something straight. I am very annoyed with myself. Why? Because I didn't check your work, not Sheila's. I trusted you to do your job properly. I now know that I can't. I now know that we are going to have a new policy. Housekeeping staff, whoever they may be, will not be allowed to sign off until their rooms have been checked by one member of the management team. It is then the responsibility of that management member if it is not done properly. Did you know, and I have only today discovered, that Sheila had another job. No? Well, let me tell you. She goes to people's houses in the afternoon, as soon as she had finished her shift here, to do ladies nails.'

Pam and Moaner look aghast at each other.

'Didn't think you knew. I also think we have given her too much responsibility, so we need to take on another housekeeper, so her days off are covered as well.'

A few days later I mentioned my misgivings to Pam about the wisdom of employing Moaner, but we both appreciated we were far too far down the employment line to do anything about it. We certainly didn't want to say anything to Mark, because his immediate reaction would have been to sack her. The US employment laws are a lot more lax than ours.

As it happened, this policy of checking rooms stood me in very good stead some eighteen months later, when I had guests to check in one of the top attic rooms. Sheila was long gone by this stage, we now had a team of three English ladies who worked together really well. Not only did someone check the rooms with housekeeping, I also went into the rooms before guests were due to arrive.

On my own, just checking, I opened the door to hear the distinctive sounds of a pigeon cooing. There it was, under the window, sitting on the nest. That was also under the window, which was open too far, enabling said bird to enter at will. I did nothing, gently closed the door, and went looking for the senior housekeeper. Without informing her why I required her company, we went together to room 25.

'Go on, how long do you think that nest has been there?'

'Don't know Harry, must be a few days.'

'And do you think that the guests checking in this afternoon would like to share their room with a pigeon and its nest?'

'Probably not.'

'So what do you think I should do with the nest?' By then the pigeon was outside the room, on the window ledge.

'Don't know.'

Very gently, I lifted the nest, and placed it outside the window, on a convenient flat roof.

***

After we had owned the Sheldon for two months, Pam and I went to California to stay with Mark and Deanna. It required a face to face visit, as we wanted to give them a complete assessment of the way things were going. It was only a week's break, just before Easter so not too many guests, we would be back in time for the influx.

Mark and I had discussed our travel arrangements, and we agreed that because the hotel was paying for our flight tickets, we would fly economy class. They collected us from Los Angeles airport in their large SUV. They lived in a gated community within a mile of the expensive coast, had been there for five years, but never had anyone to stay before. There were only about a dozen houses in the complex, no security guards on the gate, just a pass code to gain entrance. You drove into the complex, and there was the house, very large for two people.

We realised that they had few friends, Deanna was obsessed with the shopping channels and looking after a pygmy dog and aggressive cat. The house itself was on two levels, ground floor and one above. The kitchen was accessed by the door from the double garage, and was inevitably huge. The television was never turned off while we were there, except for sleeping. There was expensive kitchen equipment, it could have been straight out of a show home, but was seldom used for cooking. The lounge area was at the main part of this huge room, with a dining table as well as settees and armchairs. It was all furnished in expensive good taste.

We went out for a drive one afternoon in his Routemaster bus, saw the factory, were introduced to a very few members of staff, including Deanna's parents and sister. He also had an electric boat moored in a marina, we had a very pleasant evening going for a moonlit ride. On the Sunday lunchtime, Mark and Deanna invited all their friends round to introduce us to them, and it was a most convivial and enjoyable social occasion. They really did know some extremely pleasant people, and despite our business experience with the couple, they could be lovely people, excellent company, and we also had some great times with them, especially the earlier days.

We decided that the hotel budget would stand a three night visit to Las Vegas, which was paid for on the company credit card. Mark drove the four of us there from L.A. to Vegas, a journey of some five hours through desert and little else. The journey was fascinating, miles and miles of flat landscape stretching out into nowhere desert. The air conditioning in the car worked full blast, because when we exited mid-way for a refreshment and comfort stop the heat hit you just walking from the car to the air-conditioned restaurant.

Pam and I had been to Vegas on two previous occasions, so we were no strangers to the town. We were to have a three night stay, and our hotel was the Wynn. The Americans have a lovely phrase to describe something superior as upscale, and that was a perfect word to describe the Wynn Hotel for our March 2007 visit.

We learned some more about their personalities and choice of lifestyle, because each evening they had room service deliver their meals. She didn't drink at all, he very little maybe the occasional beer, while Pam and I enjoy a glass of quality wine, especially when on holiday. We are not gamblers either, budgeting very little for this activity. We preferred the shows, especially the free ones in the hotel lounges, whereas they didn't bother doing much, staying a lot of the time in their hotel room watching TV This was not for us. So we sneaked out all the time to appreciate the sights.

During the day we went out driving. Las Vegas is still a growing city, population over a million, and a lovely place to visit despite the gambling. The standard of restaurants is what you want it to be, which means that you can spend fortunes on celebrity chef restaurants or have a snack in a chain diner. It is as diverse as that, with the suburbs providing even more variety of activities. The shops are something else, especially with clothing, we were taken with the shoe shops. The discount ones were the best, and I bought a pair of patterned boots that almost go up to the knee for $80 on one visit.

The stay with Mark and Deanna lasted for seven days and was memorable for all the right reasons; we socialised and enjoyed each others' company; we have nothing but great memories of our time with them. They were excellent hosts, wanting to show their home life at its best and succeeding very well.

***

A month later, after Easter, Mark and Deanna came over for their fateful visit.

My marketing was already showing success, as the hotel was full, and Mark and I had our first row when he insisted he and Deanna were entitled to have one of the executive rooms in the lower ground floor. I was adamant that I wasn't going to bump a paying guest. It was pathetically childish, each obdurate. Compromise had to be found, so without telling him I found a more expensive hotel for the guest. I reckon that stay cost the Sheldon about £2,000, with lost revenue and paying the extra to the other hotel.

The conversation went something like this.

'Mark, you do realise that your little stay and petulance has cost the Sheldon in the region of £2,000, what with lost revenue from the room and paying all that extra to the Devonshire.'

'So what, I deserve it, as the owner of the Sheldon.'

'Part owner, and as the operating director you should bow to my viewpoint.'

'As the sleeping partner with more invested what I say goes.'

'So there's no discussion to be had, then.'

This conversation was held over lunch the first day that they arrived. We had shown return courtesy by meeting them at Gatwick Airport, about an hours' drive from the south coast.

The next morning, after breakfast, we had the meeting in the hotel lounge with accountant, bank, and solicitor.

***

The Aftermath

It was during this visit that Mark had a word with our book-keeper Trish. We didn't know about this for a long time afterwards, she is such a good, loyal, friend, and wanted to spare us knowing what was occurring.

We had no idea that he had even had a chat with her, but it was a private one. She told us how the conversation went.

'As you are the book keeper, you are in a pretty privileged position to know what's going on. I would prefer to keep this confidential between the two of us, but would appreciate keeping in contact, so you let me know what's really happening in the hotel. You know, if you are not comfortable with what's occurring, perhaps you could let me know?'

Trish 'So you would prefer Harry didn't know about this arrangement.'

'Yes.'

'But you are placing me in a pretty uncomfortable position.'

'Why?'

'We are friends.'

'That shouldn't make any difference. You see, what I am asking is for the good of the hotel. There would be no comeback on you, no-one would ever know it was you, all I am asking is a quiet word if you think, shall we say, that the hotel isn't being run quite as you would like it to be, and I could do something about it.'

Trish 'No, sorry, it's not something I want to be involved with.'

Mark and Deanna returned to California after their week with us, we socialised with them, even having a meal one evening at the Mirabelle Restaurant at The Grand Hotel. Of course, the Sheldon credit card paid for that. Deanna didn't drink, neither did Mark as usual, the atmosphere wasn't nearly as convivial as it could have been, because Pam and I were privately discussing our future.

We were stuck. Here we were, getting on a bit, all our capital tied up in a business that was based on very rocky foundations, with a partner who was a plank, immature, and who could potentially leave us in the lurch by walking away if he wanted to. We may have been equal partners, but the ownership of the property made him the senior one, as he had placed more money into it. This was a period of uncertainty for us, as we also had a private word with the accountant when they had returned. His advice was gloomy. Sit it out and hope for the best.

We asked the accountant for his frank advice. He was fully aware of the friendship between us, possibly being even more aghast at Mark's revelation at the business meeting.

'I don't know if you fully appreciate the ramifications of what Mark said,' he told us. 'When you borrow a hundred grand on credit cards, the interest isn't just astronomical, it is also creating its own pressures. They manifest in your everyday life, because you know you can't exist without the money to support the paybacks. That is why he will be grouchy, unreasonable, very likely irrational in business decisions, and you will have to be very careful with the way that you deal with Mark.' He paused. 'Just saying, watch your back and hope for the best. But allow for the worst. Be prepared.'

Chapter Five: Suggestions

Moaner had come from a health service background, and apparently one of the things that management liked to specialise in was how to improve. She had a 'brilliant' idea that she, Pam and I should all write down what annoyed us, so we could then have a meeting with the staff and make improvements. I have no idea what happened to the other copies, or even if they were ever written, but I still have on computer my list, and I reproduce it here

What Annoys Me

Restaurant

- Cups on the tables all the time. These should be stored, and placed on table when tea/coffee ordered at end of evening meal
- Cutlery should be cleaned properly. At present, it is only cursorily checked when placed on table.
- Mat outside kitchen door. It just annoys me, but other than chucking it away, don't know solution.
- Re-design restaurant so tables are not so close to kitchen door.

Kitchen

- Men talking too loudly when Guests can hear in restaurant. Radio is fine.
- Oil swinging door.
- Hook on back kitchen door to keep it open in warm weather.

- Ceiling is filthy and needs washing and then painting white.

- Sliding door cupboards above water heater need to be kept shut, and clean – very high up above it so this is not being done at present.

- Sweep under ALL cupboards etc every day, and before kitchen staff go home after breakfast wash walls and floors

Public areas

- Stairs are not cleaned frequently enough.

- Papers are not removed from lounge before Guests come down in morning. Bins are not always emptied, and new bags replace full ones. Exceptional, I know, but one three day period about a month ago main bin not emptied at all.

- Public toilets not always cleaned every day. This should be essential.

- Has anyone ever climbed up to clean TV in bar?

- Downstairs office not cleaned on a regular basis.

- Chairs should be moved when hoovering in bar and lounge area. At present, only lounge appears to be hoovered on any frequent basis.

- Housekeeping staff should inform M in advance when they require heavy lifting – not always possible, I know, but should be possible to anticipate more than it is.

Some of these topics are pretty obvious, but let me explain a little more...

Restaurant

It used to really bug me that the tea/coffee cups were on the table all the time. It made the restaurant look like a café, and we were trying to improve. For some strange reason, Poles love to have cups and saucers on view all the time. Perhaps it's a National identity thing, you know, proud of your crockery, but hard as I tried, and paying their wages, I failed in my endeavours to make them comply with my simple request.

Cutlery. Now come on, how difficult is it to check the cutlery as you put it on the table? It's come out of a boiling hot washer, and all I wanted was for them to have a good look. Yes, I did succeed here, but only because I banged on and on about it, and checked the restaurant every night and threw stained cutlery into the sink.

There was a swing door from the restaurant into the kitchen for hygiene, and the mat was replaced under contract every few days. At that meeting it was explained to me (slowly because sometimes even I could be a bit dim) that under hygiene regulations there should be a mat to take up the spillage as the door was opened. I simply asked the question 'Why is anything spilled from the plate? Don't you take sufficient care when carrying the plates?'

The poor diners who were close to the kitchen could hear everything going on, and if we didn't like anyone then they were allocated those tables. The staff wanted those allocated first, so they didn't have to carry the spilled food so far. I referred to it as the 'naughty corner'.

Kitchen

Okay, I could just about tolerate a radio in the kitchen, they need something to relieve the tedium of cooking, but when they are serving then that's different. YOU DON'T HAVE TO SHOUT was a constant cry. It they had a row in Polish, then Pam, Moaner or I had to be on it immediately, because some of our better educated guests could actually understand Polish sometimes, and that's the lady guests as well as the men guests.

The swinging door needed constant oiling, as it was for ever being swung back on its hinges. How long did it take an assistant cook to flow some 3 in 1 oil? I was buying it, for goodness sake.

They had windows in the kitchen, as well as a back door. Assistant cook was also a handyman, and quite capable of fitting a catch on the swing door to keep it open while they were creating culinary masterpieces. Did he ever do it? What do you think. It was their discomfort, so I never pushed this point.

Who looks up when they enter a restaurant kitchen? I did, and didn't like what I saw. A couple of times a year, when we weren't very busy, I would buy the paint, and they were very careful (I think) not to drop any into the home made soup.

We put them through their food preparation course, no cost to them, and part of this was maintaining the manual showing that they had done all in the kitchen that they were supposed to. That included sweeping under the cupboards and lower levels (without any food being on preparation surfaces). Amazing how much you have to hold peoples' hands to ensure common sense. As Pam always tells me.

Public areas

We employed a night porter, what the hell was he doing to earn his crust? Make sure that the lounge is nice and tidy when the first guest comes down in the morning. Not rocket science, and it took a long time for me to get this point across. I ended up dumping the old newspapers on the night porter's bed, and then he got the message.

Okay, who would want to climb up to have a look at the top of the TV in the lounge that was on a wall bracket about seven feet up. To see if it had been dusted. Risk assessment for the housekeeping staff would likely reject this idea of mine, and Moaner with her health service background didn't think much of the idea, and I quietly dropped it. Can't be right all the time.

Okay, it was my mess, my office, and my responsibility to keep the office clean. Okay, they laughed at this suggestion, and I had the good grace to laugh along with them. Through gritted teeth.

This is a stupid suggestion to make – I am implying that we employ heavy staff who require assistance with elevating themselves.

The meeting went fine, very productive, and a few weeks later we had a shorter meeting where the staff made suggestions of things that annoyed them. I soon shot that one down.

Chapter Six: All About Experiences with Guests

The previous owners when purchasing the hotel about three years before us had initially lived in the lower ground floor rooms, converting them into guest accommodation at great expense. They had mainly done a good job, but as the rooms were lower level, were prone to flooding if really heavy rain occurred.

Spring time, and the hotel was about three quarters full. Most hotels struggle with full occupancy on a Sunday night, because it's not easy to find guests wanting to stay a Sunday if they come for the weekend, but we provided ours with evening meals, and three and four nights and longer breaks, with special rates, so our occupancy rate was pretty good. We had managed to get away by lunch time, so were looking forward to a relaxing afternoon doing not particularly much, maybe a stroll along the seafront, perhaps a cup of coffee with a drop of brandy in it, or possibility an ice cream cone with a chocolate flake. Lots of simple things to anticipate, and we had been back at our flat about ten minutes' walk away from the hotel, when the heavens opened. It was such heavy rain that the roads were flooded, and we wondered how the hotel would cope. Badly.

The phone went, it was the duty Polish manager.

'We have a problem.'

I came to dread those words, because it usually meant that I would have to show some kind of DIY. initiative, leadership, and taking control of the whole situation. Strange when there is something wrong how others tended to look to me for guidance, and this was no exception.

'What's wrong? Is it the rain?'

'Yes, we're flooded out downstairs. Sorry to bother you on your afternoon off but I think you'd better return.'

On went the heavy wet gear, and we ventured out. By the time we were at the end of our road it had stopped raining, and the sun was coming out. Off came the raincoat, and it was a brisk walk along the seafront to the hotel. It was apparent when we looked downstairs that two of the superior rooms that had been converted by the previous owner plus the corridor were flooded, requiring immediate attention. The guests were out, so the first thing we did was clear the leaves from the drain in the car park, and I had to wade through about two feet of water, and then roll my sleeve up as far as it could go and plunge my hand into the drain to remove the cover with leaves. That was the easy part. Then it was back to the corridor, and organise buckets and mops. The staff were very amenable, and then it was into the rooms to see how bad it was. Fortunately, the water had only got as far as the bathroom door in each room, and there were no belongings on the floor, but the rooms were uninhabitable, so we then had to organise the staff to check that two rooms upstairs were ready for immediate occupation.

Back on the phone to the mobiles of the two guests.

'Hello, Mr and Mrs. ..? It's Harry here from the Sheldon. Yes, it did rain, didn't it? Hope you didn't get too wet. Oh, you were hiding under the pier at the time. Well, the rain has managed to get through the door into the corridor outside your bedroom, and a little bit into your room. Your carpet is all wet, and of course we can't get a humidifier on a Sunday. We have another room available upstairs, and would like to carry everything upstairs for you. Would it be okay if we packed everything, or would you like to come back to do it yourself? Yes, we will take extra care. Okay, have a good afternoon. Thanks. Bye'

I spoke to the staff. 'Pack up everything, and take it upstairs. Pam and I will give you a hand.'

Very carefully, we packed up everything, and checked that the drawers and cupboards were empty of all belongings. One of the guests had a laptop, and when I went to place it in its case

I noticed that there were some DVDs at the bottom. Of course, rather than squash and potentially damage them, I took them out. Wow!!!! Hard naughty stuff, and this couple were well into their sixties. Pam looked over.

'What's that?'

Now come on reader, what would you do in those circumstances? I showed them to her.

'Wow, they look really interesting.'

Whoo, that wasn't the response I was expecting. I gently took them from her and placed them back in the case with the laptop. When the guests returned later and we gave them the keys to their new room, we all managed to keep a straight face. Don't know how.

The Walking Party

Unfortunately, Mark wanted to alter a lot, including the spending pattern of the guests. He was too thick to appreciate that before you could attempt this course of action, you had to provide the 'improved' guest with a superior standard of accommodation. Impossible without spending vast sums of money, which of course none of us had, so we were stuck with the same type of lovely guest that traditionally stayed in our hotel. Pam and I were very comfortable with that state of affairs, because we knew from experience from owning our executive chauffeur hire business that if you improved the business, the standard of client didn't necessarily follow. Americans can be lovely people, we know that because some of them might be reading this book even as you are, but when they travel they can be a pain in the bum. The worst revue I ever had at the hotel was posted on Trip Advisor by an American guest who blatantly lied about me. If I had done what she said I did, then she would have been justified in going straight to the local police station, but she didn't, because it was lies. However, most of our guests came as couples, or pairs, and we rarely enjoyed groups. Except for the walkers.

A group of between thirty and forty people came for the same week every year in the Spring, to enjoy rambling and walking along the south coast of England. Our location was ideal for this, as the town's position is at the foot of a well-known beauty spot, at the beginning of the South Downs Way, and has lots of lovely extras like four theatres, pier, and seafront Carpet Gardens.

Their age group was from sixty to a lot older, and they were demanding. I don't just mean demanding, I mean seriously extra special demanding. We had only owned the hotel for four months when they came calling, and by mid-way through their week the staff were in tears, some of the party were on the verge of walking out on us refusing to pay, and I could have found it very easy to pin both male and female ringleaders against a wall and suggest that to continue breathing they would have to change their ways to such an extent that on their return their nearest and dearest would find them unrecognisable. But back to the beginning of their stay.

They came every year, and in correspondence we had assured them that all was as before, no changes from the previous management, and the only thing they would notice was different faces. Comfort zone expectations were to be maintained, and as they had previously visited they knew the layout of the hotel's rooms, so allocated themselves. We had already discovered that this area could be a minefield, and more of this later. Our group had a new leader, as the previous one was very unwell, and subsequently passed on just before their arrival, which created quite an initial dampener. The best downstairs rooms were snaffled by the organiser and his little coterie, which went down fine with the others. They all had their comfort zones, and we had also provided them with menu listings before their arrival so they could approve. So far so good, but the biggest problem that was to initially arise was the fact that we plated the food in the kitchen.

You may recall that our chef at home in Poland had been a teacher, and her partner who was her assistant and washer-up a graphic designer and amateur photographer, so they were learning on the job. Our general manager Moaner had been an office manager with no hotel experience, and my wife and I had previously run a six bedroom guest house. We were all (okay, maybe with the exception of Moaner) keen to learn and get it right, and in the four months before the arrival of the walkers had mainly achieved customer success. That was to change dramatically.

They travelled from the same part of the country in separate vehicles, and we had been furnished with the room allocation list by The Leader. As usual, I escorted them to their rooms, carrying their luggage, and all was okay until we served their first evening meal. They wanted the vegetables in separate dishes so they could help themselves. Now we did not have a policy of dictating to our guests what they would have, in what form, and when, but we did think that this request was more than a little unreasonable. No-one said anything at this stage, but it didn't help that it was raining heavily, and they could not ramble in as much comfort as they desired. Fair weather walkers to my mind. I had bought in a barrel of beer for the bar in expectation of bumper takings, but they failed to materialise. A sober-sided lot who took their pleasures seriously, and during the whole week the bar itself took less than £200, even though they did buy the odd bottle of wine that bumped up profits a bit, and two of the ladies sat in the bar all evening nursing their schooners of sherry over their bowl of free peanuts.

Pam and I went out on the second night to a hotel association dinner, and were called back by the lady chef who was in tears. That was unusual behaviour from her, as her partner was known to be sulky and volatile, and Pam discovered what arsehole was in Polish. We remember dupek to this day. Oh yes, zva is two, and whooshka is spoon (I think that is the correct spelling, but you get the meaning).

'They don't like my food. They sent it back.'

'What was wrong with it?' we asked calmly.

'They said it wasn't plain enough, they wanted more choice.'

We found The Leader and Mrs. Leader, and asked them their viewpoint.

'We wanted to have more choice.'

'But we discussed the menus before you came, We are providing you with exactly what we agreed. Do you want to alter the menus for future evenings?'

'No,' said Mrs Leader. 'We don't like the vegetables coming up on the plate. We are used to them being on separate serving dishes.'

I said to Pam 'Have we got those serving dishes in the top cupboard?'

'Yes', she replied.

'Problem number one solved. Now, what's wrong with the menus?'

'It's not the menus themselves, it's the actual cooking.'

I am going to pause a moment here, and give you a little background about Pam and myself. Aged about sixty, we were used to dealing with the public for many years, but not letting them get away with anything we considered unreasonable. I do think that I have some rough edges, and can be caustic sometimes which doesn't go down too well. Pam is the peace maker, lovely personality, and always wants a quiet life. However, don't wind her up unnecessarily, because pacifism can disappear. We both thought that this group of people were being unreasonable, without giving us any sensible cause for complaint, but they were worth quite a few thousands to us when we really needed it, and we wanted them to return for years to come. So tact was required, not confrontation.

'Can you be more precise in your area of unhappiness with the cooking please,' I started. 'Is it too salty? Is it over cooked? Is it undercooked? Is there sufficient variety of menu? You can see our dilemma here, and we need your input. It's no good just saying that you're not enjoying the food. You have to be more specific in your comments for us to do something about it to your satisfaction.'

Pam was nodding in agreement throughout this. The chef and her partner were sulking in the kitchen, refusing to go home, and likely going to mutiny about cooking for this lot ever again. I certainly didn't fancy cooking 45 breakfasts the next morning.

'We would like three choices for starters, four main courses, and three sweets.'

Now I knew we were getting somewhere. I looked at Pam. 'Can I suggest a different homemade soup every day, a conventional fruit juice, and a starter such as cheese soufflé, or mushroom tart. Then main course of roast, fish, salad, or omelette, and to finish fruit salad, or something like that. Is this a menu that we can work to?'

Mr and Mrs Leader nodded, as did Pam. 'And I would suggest that we get the serving vegetable dishes down from the top cupboard, we might even wash them, and then use them every night.' Fortunately Mr and Mrs Leader still retained their sense of humour, as they didn't want to abandon their holiday for another hotel. 'We want to compromise and still ensure that your stay is an enjoyable as possible'. Pam and the audience nodded some more.

So, it was back into the lounge to speak to the walkers who were sipping their sherries and half pints of under-priced bitter and eating the free peanuts (have I mentioned the free peanuts already? Sorry to be boring) to let them know what was occurring. Then into the kitchen to placate the staff. Not so easy, and Pam came into her most tactful self here. 'There there, it's all right, yes, they are nasty people, yes, we are not used to dealing with such ingratitude, and they'll only be here for a few more days and then we'll be rid of them. And no, you can't spit in their food.'

The upshot of this incident meant that we learned a lot more about how to deal with the guests, and more especially the staff. We must have done a good job, because when they left they booked for next year already, there were so many smiles and happy people, and the tip box was quite full. Now there's another area of contention.

The Rotarians

What a lovely group. Just like the walkers, they were a repeat group. Rotary held an annual conference in Eastbourne, and as our hotel was quite close to the conference venue, seafront, and town centre, it was a logical choice to stay. Again, the organiser took the best rooms for themselves, but we had no complaints because all our rooms were very presentable. Okay, not the height of luxury maybe, but very high standards, especially the cleaning, now the housekeeping problems had been eradicated.

Our group of Rotarians came from North London, being about forty in number. In a previous career I had been based very close to them, and we had some mutual acquaintances. They were all business people, some retired, all ages as well as social groups, a lot of couples with quite a few singles as well. The leading group were determined to enjoy and appreciate their break to the maximum, which involved copious amounts of alcoholic consumption. This group provided us with the best bar take during our hotel ownership.

I usually had three varieties of Sherry, and two of Port in stock, but guessed their background so went to the wine merchant located at the rear of the Grand Hotel. They had some very good quality port at about £30 a bottle, which is a lot of money to pay. However, the quality was superb, so I decanted slowly, keeping the bottle to prove the content. I bought three bottles, taking a chance they would be sold.

A bottle of fortified wine represents excellent profitability for a retailer such as me, with sixteen measures each time. I charged £3 a glass usually, upping it to £6 as it was such a lovely quality. After two nights, they had gone, so I returned for another three, which was the end of that bin.

The organiser was a man with a great sense of humour, with one of the single ladies in the party being a mature person in her late sixties. She was glamorous, a successful businesswoman, wealthy, very presentable, and a lovely personality. Also in the group was a visitor from New York. This man was in his late twenties, the son of a successful entrepreneur, visiting London on a learning business trip for a month. He was a late addition to the party, included in all the activities, especially the bar. Each room ran a bar tab, signing a book each time, the young American wasn't allowed to pay for anything. They got him badly drunk on port the first night.

He had never tried the delicious liquid previously, immediately appreciating the fine flavour and quality. Yes, he was sipping it, initially sniffing the aroma, but that soon went as he quaffed all the more. Of course, the older men encouraged this indulgent behaviour, knowing full well how bad his hangover would be the next morning. We didn't see him for breakfast, he only just arrived in time to attend the conference.

That night found him more circumspect in the bar, going out for dinner instead of our dining room, and when he returned he was in the company of a small group. He was the first to leave the party at midnight, which was of course no surprise to those of who have previously imbibed port in quantity to our ultimate cost. The rest retired about 2am, I served the last of them, and was still up for breakfast the next morning. It was my job to be present.

There was some speculation about various people in the larger group swapping rooms during the night, sharing with people who were not their usual partners. The strongest rumour which turned out to be fact concerned the young American and the single business lady. They were to spend the next two nights in one room. The Eastbourne visit transpired to be a memorable one all round.

The Huge Man

Another local hotel held bridge tournaments. Unfortunately, The Sheldon's configuration was not conducive, with limited public areas, so it was impossible for us to hold any kind of tournament or gathering. However, we did manage to accommodate overflows. We had four single men stay with us who were bridge players. One man was fine, no problems, one man was unpleasant, poor manners really, but not much else was wrong with him.

The third man managed to be ill all over his bathroom. Housekeeping serviced his room to discover he had been sick over the walls, the floor, inside the shower. The room had to be taken out of action of course, he was billed a hefty service charge, but I suppose it was his arrogance we disliked. He never said a word, just waited for it to be discovered. How can anyone have such disregard for hotel staff opinion I don't know, and this was not a unique occurrence during our ownership. But it was guest number four who was the objectionable one for quite a few reason. Firstly, it was his size.

How people look doesn't bother me at all. During our ownership, we served all manner of different looking people, from those handicapped (always lovely and polite), very small (absolutely delightful) to such a variety of skin hues it was a genuine pleasure to welcome them all to the Sheldon. We accommodated large guests on many occasions, but this man just didn't know how to behave in public.

I am not going to dwell on his size, even though it is somewhat relevant to his behaviour. He had to sit on two chairs in the dining room, as he was getting on for forty stone by the look of him. The only thing he didn't do was click his fingers at the restaurant staff, but he would bellow in a stentorian tone

'BRING ME SOME YOGHURT AND CEREAL.

The first morning, he said to Pam 'I want scrambled eggs. You DO know how to cook scrambled eggs, don't you? No milk, just salt and pepper and butter.'

All the other guests were looking askance during every altercation, they didn't appreciate his lack of manners and respect to hotel staff. He was with us for three days, and during this time housekeeping said that the shower had not been used. Mind you, it would have been impossible for him to have fitted inside the cubicle. He looked unclean, his clothes looked unkempt, and of all the guests who stayed with us he and his party were the worst of the lot.

Chapter Seven: Plans

The Summer months passed pretty fast for us. I reported to Mark on a daily basis, bookings, prospects, what was occurring in the Eastbourne business community. We got into a routine pretty fast, the staff were mainly loyal, mostly Polish with lovely manners to the guests, and professional in their attitude. The housekeeper decided one day at short notice to resign, the nails were paying more of course without so much effort, but I was still surprised because she was able to legitimise her salary with us, and gain cash with the afternoon business.

We didn't replace her with a Polish person this time, but placed an advert in the local paper. We were inundated with replies, and without me sitting on the interviews two English ladies were engaged. They were both lovely.

Mark was onto me all the time for the £6,000 to be transferred across to his bank each month, the accountant was telling me that we couldn't afford it for much longer, something was going to break, and he was worried it might be the finances.

I wanted to increase the hours we were able to open the bar, so filled in the planning application form. It was a pretty straightforward procedure. You stated the hours you wanted to open, the times that music was to be played to the public, and then the application was publicly posted for all to see, as well as in the local newspaper. However, I had no idea the furore this was to create.

The hotel is situated in an area of Eastbourne called the Lower Meads. There is also The Meads, but our part is closer to the seafront, hence the lower, not implying that those from this area were of the lower class, despite the fact that they were probably condescended by those living up the hill.

Just as a little anecdote, the population of Eastbourne is just over 100,000, with the average age 37. There is a smaller area in The Meads that has a population of 1,300, and their average age is 73.

Anyway, Lower Meads came out in force to object to our plans.

The planning committee of Eastbourne council met at 6:30pm. It was a very large room in the council offices building, designed for meetings, with a crescent designed table with the three councillors ready to sit in judgment, their clerks at an adjacent table, with the public facing them. About forty chairs were laid out in rows, however on most occasions very few people attended. Not so for the Sheldon's application.

Every chair was occupied, however as there were only two applications on the agenda they all thought they were in for an early evening. Wrong. The other applicant was a local restaurant, established many years, who wanted to vary his opening hours, and he was aghast that there were so many objectors. He need not have worried, they were all there for me. The clerk soon discovered this, so ensured that we were second and last in the running order.

After ten minutes deliberations, the councillors passed his without any amendments. Then it was my turn.

Unknown to me, three apartment blocks had organised petitions against the extension of the hours whereby the hotel could sell alcohol. Their vehemence however was even more for the increase of hours that we could play music to the public. You would have thought that I wanted to open a jazz club in the bar selling a menu of illegal substances at all hours to people of all ages. Their vitriol was personal, nasty, illogical, something that was completely unwarranted.

For example, they questioned my suitability to be a licence holder. This from people who knew nothing about me, had never met me, would pass me in the street without acknowledgement. They regarded me as trade, someone not from their class, if I had been Meads born and bred, attended Eastbourne College, moved in their circles, it would have been entirely different. The objectors were all aged over sixty, mainly ladies.

Of course, they really got my back up, but I couldn't show this because I had to have an image of a reasonable hotelier listening to the neighbourhood concerns. I disseminated their arguments, then before my plans were kicked out completely suggested a compromise. Sunday to Thursday evening hours to be curtailed to 11pm, Friday and Saturday midnight. I didn't really want any more in any case, I had only asked for the extra hours just in case. The time was now 9:30pm, we had been back and forth for two and a half hours, the councillors and staff wanted to go home, so they immediately jumped on my ideas, agreed, and that was that.

Did I ever have functions that lasted late? Of course not, all my guests wanted was an early night. The Sheldon wasn't really a hotel that leant itself to functions. But that wasn't the point, was it?

***

I went to business breakfasts twice a week, one with the chamber of commerce, another with a very intense group who tried to make you give as many introductions to your fellow members as possible. It would be very silly of me to name this group, but my description I suspect might be sufficient to identify if you have ever been invited. I had been a member for some three months, and gained absolutely zero recommendations. Every week they came round the room asking for the slips with details of the referrals, but none ever came my way. The last part of the meeting involved standing up and passing them on, and when it came to my turn I simply stated

'I have three referrals this week, one for _, one for _, and one for _. However, as usual, I have received none, and I wonder if you know what I do. I stand here every week and give you my sixty second presentation, I network with you all before and after the meeting, I sit next to you and tell you about my week, but do you

REALLY know about my hotel? Because if you say you do, then I am pretty hacked off that week after week I pass round these slips of paper and get nothing in return.'

It went very quiet.

El Presidente said 'It might be best if we spoke about this in private.'

'Fine by me, but the message is still the same. Have a chat at your committee meeting when we're finished, and then come back to me.'

There was a phone call later on that morning from the man in charge. He sounded awkward, and his tone was one of annoyance that I had raised this matter at an open meeting.

'Harry, we are concerned that you are not happy. At next week's meeting I am suggesting that the person who was going to do their ten minute presentation delay it for a week so you can do yours.'

'Well, that's a start. What else?'

'Now come on, we're making an effort here. We've listened to what you have said, and are doing our best.'

'Shame that it took me standing up like that to get a reaction, though. I know that you analyse who receives the most referrals, my zero should have been flagged up a long time ago. Yes, I will do the ten minute, and also ask you to make a special mention next week that my hotel needs as much business as possible.'

Next week, I had my presentation very well prepared, and I thought that it went down very well. So well in fact that one of the members, a car salesman, asked me privately

'Harry, any chance of you letting me have a room for a couple of hours next Tuesday afternoon? I need to have a special conference, and a private hotel room would be ideal.'

I knew that this man was married, and it would take some swinging past Pam, but a pal had asked a favour, and I wanted to get as much business as possible. I said yes.

Next Tuesday he came for his private conference, and stayed with his colleague for a couple of hours. With grateful thanks he left, and it was funny really, but we got a lot more business recommendations for the rest of my membership of this club. Can't think why.

***

The four executive basement rooms also had a small suite at one end, consisting the night porter's room, his shower and toilet room, which were accessed through the office. This was a small, less than ten foot square airless windowless room, the main feature being the floor safe. That barked your legs if you were unwary, it was probably three feet square, impossible to move to re-design the office, and we had to be very careful not to lose the only long metal key. Behind one office wall was the lift mechanism, only accessed from the outside. We had four security cameras outside the hotel and inside reception, so you could watch these from the wall mounted screens. I often used to nod off sitting in my chair.

There is a local wholesale cash and carry business, but with added VAT it was often cheaper to purchase from the larger supermarkets on discount. An average bottle of spirits for example whisky, gin, vodka, will realise 32 measures. A bottle can cost about £12, sometimes a litre £15 on discount, and at £2.50 – £3 a measure there is a lot of profit to be made. Likewise with the wine.

The Eastbourne wine merchant trade for the restaurants and hotels as well as pubs is monopolised by one firm, who are family run and extremely efficient. They deliver at short notice, so were a pleasure to deal with. I had a basic wine list of eight white and eight red, with some rose and bubbles on offer as well. I purchased a huge fridge at a very reasonable price, keeping it stocked with the white which was very popular. I worked on a retail price of three times the purchase, which is not at all greedy but very good on our turnover. The bar business was excellent, but knackering in the evening.

We tended to stay until eight, eating dinner at the same time as the guests, slowly walking along the seafront hand in hand, falling asleep very quickly when we went to bed. I hadn't really appreciated before we started just how tiring the hotel business is, hands on all the time, potentially difficult customers, staff that required frequent mollycoddling, and authorities that couldn't be put off. One such person was the public health inspector.

At the time this tale is set, about 2006-2008, there were three such people in their department, but we somehow managed to get the same one every time. He had a reputation of being a complete and utter bastard, wanting to find fault and disappointed when failing, but strangely he seemed to take to the Sheldon, and we always had the best relationship with him.

He would arrive usually by appointment, but sometimes without, remove his outdoor garments, donning a white coat and hat, almost looking like a cricket umpire. All that was missing was a knitted Arran sweater tied around his waist. Clipboard in hand, he would examine every surface, cupboard, oven, fridge, storage, never showing any emotion. Don't play cards with this man. Thermometer in hand, he had free range. I always hid in my office while this performance was being enacted, leaving it to Pam and Moaner. The chef and her partner were in the kitchen throughout.

There was a maximum score possible of 23, we never achieved that, but every single time came very close. Every day the kitchen staff had to complete a form stating that they had inspected, cleaned, and were satisfied that all had been completed to the highest standards. Just occasionally they forgot, and that's what let us down, but we always gained the maximum for everything else, so that is why I suppose he was so pleased with us.

I was still reporting to Mark and Deanna on a daily basis, explaining what had been done, how well it had been done, and by who. But we were already discussing the future. Or lack of it.

***

Tennis was first played at a Wimbledon tournament in 1877. It was first played at Devonshire Park, Eastbourne, in 1880. The week before Wimbledon, the town of Eastbourne is taken over by tennis fans.

Until recently this was an annual tournament just for professional lady players, but of late has an open draw for the male players as well. The prize money is not bad, it is an official Lawn Tennis Association tournament, with officials provided by the governing body. The stewards and assistants are provided from local students, as there are many educational establishments in the town. The kids love it, because they get to see some really big names.

The tickets go on sale four months in advance, with some days selling out really quickly. The qualification rounds occur the first Saturday, when admission is free for the public. The tournament proper starts on the first Monday, final played on Saturday. There is a web site, with order of play published daily, so it is possible to download and print ready for guests when they come down for breakfast. We at the Sheldon always did, so did all the establishments that were clued up. Some didn't bother, which speaks volumes for their abilities to provide their guests with what was required.

If you aren't full during the tennis week, then you are never going to be. Strangely, only about half our trade that week was for the tennis, other guests were for their stay regardless. Evening meal trade was hit and miss, because play may continue until 8pm. These guests were devoted tennis fans, thinking nothing of staying until the last ball was hit and the last volley was lost. A lot of the guests were of a sapphic background, always ideal guests. My definition of an ideal guest is one who never complains, appreciating the superb standard of service provided by yours truly and his team. We had the order of play ready every morning, we booked restaurants, we had free nuts on the bar, we provided ice buckets to keep the wine cool, we were really geared up to provide a high standard.

The only fly in the ointment came when the weather turned inclement. Then they were bored. Mind you, the sandwich trade for lunches did well if play was delayed until mid afternoon. We used to provide packed lunches because the price of food inside the grounds is so high. We all liked the tennis week, not just because we were full, but because of the type of guest. They were all lovely.

Chapter Eight: Prospects

I was trying to get some plans out of Mark. How was his business doing? Was he doing better? Did he still require all that money to be sent every month? How did he view the future of the hotel?

What concerned me was the way he would frequently change his mind. Sometimes he was positive about the future, next year

'Harry we can start looking at the next hotel.'

Or on another occasion he would say that he was doing badly and might have to place the hotel on the market. I had to forcefully and tactfully remind him that he was playing with three people's lives – Pam, me, and Aunty Joan. Not to mention those of the hotel staff, who were committing their future in our hands.

A lot of the time I felt insecurity. We were into the hotel ownership for six months and here he was talking about selling, without consulting me first to boot. He regarded me as an employee, not partner, he could never seem to get his head around our financial arrangement. He was hooked up to me, like it or not. I am a pretty even tempered sort of person, but like many other people, if you wind me up, then I have a habit of reacting, sometimes badly, and that was what was occurring between Mark and me. Pam is a traditional peacemaker, typical Libran she assures me, calming the pair of us down. It was an easy summer, until Mark and Deanna came over in the September for their second visit.

I collected them from Heathrow, the journey was nice and relaxed, but I could somehow sense something underlying I couldn't place my finger on. They were over for a week, returning via London for an overnight stay at the Savoy Hotel. He was continuing with his grand lifestyle, despite being based on sand. That news was to come.

For many years Pam and I had enjoyed a day trip to the northern French coast, either through the tunnel or on the ferry. Sometimes I drove, sometimes we took seats with a local coach company. The day trip for Mark and Deanna and Pam and I was to be on the coach for a day trip to Le Touquet.

This is a delightful little town about an hours' drive south along the coast from Calais. We know the area very well, so were anticipating a great day out, showing our friends the sights. We were away by 7am, through the tunnel nice and quick, late morning found us sitting outside a pavement café enjoying the atmosphere. They wanted to shop. We went into a gents' outfitters, one of the most expensive he could find because it is a pricey town in any case, and he bought a Panama hat for 200 Euros. Pam and I couldn't believe he could spend so much money on one hat.

Deanna bought some delightful perfume, and then it was time for lunch. Of course, this was paid for on the company credit card, entertaining clients as the excuse, we had a fabulous long lunch. Then it was back buying more clothing, this time it was a leather belt for 50 Euros. Must have been a bloody good belt.

The coach was waiting for us, we weren't the last ones on but not far off, but it was during the 45 minutes standing in front of the coach parked on the train inside the tunnel that he made some revelations.

He casually mentioned that his two brothers and one of his two sisters had all been inside a US prison at one time or another. Their crimes were mostly the same. Bank robbery. Only he and one sister hadn't served time.

What! My business partner was part of a family of felons!

'What about Deanna?'

'Oh no, she's been nothing to do with the family business.'

Now I knew he had no sense of humour, also appreciating the fact that he was almost teetotal, so I knew instinctively he was telling the truth. Go on, what would you have said in the circumstances? Would you have said

'What, were you the getaway driver?'

***

But Mark hadn't finished there.

'My business is doing so bad that I won't be able to last until Christmas. I'm going to have to put the Sheldon on the market.'

The rest of the coach journey was spent in stunned silence, while I whispered to Pam what he had just imparted. The selling the hotel bit, not the America's Most Wanted. That was going to have to wait.

We spoke little to them for the next couple of days, wanting to let their news settle down a bit. Over dinner however, I raised the subject again, this time so the two ladies could be privy.

'So Mark, how bad is it really for you in California? Will you honestly struggle to last until Christmas? Why don't you sell your motorhome. That looked pretty good when I saw it parked up, you never use it, that should make quite a few dollars.'

'I'm not selling that, we like to get away in it as often as we can.'

'And the last time you did that was???'

'It's not up for discussion. We are not affecting our lifestyle, we will sell the hotel. It's not as if we have a partnership agreement, so I can do as I like.'

'So you expect us to give up everything we have worked for, invested all our life's work, live in rented accommodation for the rest of our lives, have no job because at our age we are unemployable, no savings, no prospects, just because you are a little bored with your little Eastbourne toy. Oh dear, it's not giving you the instant return that you dreamed of, it's actually going to have to have some time and patience devoted to it. I wonder who's doing that at present? That's right, Pam and me.'

'No need to be like that, I am only telling you what's going to happen.'

'I don't think so. Have a word with our solicitor, he'll put you straight. But let me be straight with you. Stop treating Pam and me as employees. We are not. We are partners. We trusted you, stop even thinking this way.'

Our reaction was one of horror, I had to be civil to the man, but I was rapidly losing all respect for him as a person, even less as a businessman, and was extremely annoyed with myself for being in this precarious position. We were going to have to be very firm with him and his stupid ideas.

***

We had known Jean and Clive (again, not real names, but sufficiently close for them to be anonymous) for many years. They had worked together, our friendship had been very close, so it was a natural development to introduce them to Mark and Deanna.

Clive was involved in a local bus museum as a volunteer vehicle restorer, had a licence to drive buses, liked country music with the line dancing, so it was natural that not only did we socialise for dancing, but we also went out together as a foursome quite a lot. He worked for us for a while as a part time driver, the clients liked him, so he took Mark quite a few times when they came over on social trips.

On one memorable evening, Clive was out driving one of our chauffeured clients in London. He was outside an expensive restaurant, just waiting, chatting to another driver. Clive was explaining about the volume of sight-seeing we did, the number of clients we took on day-long trips, the other driver was on more mundane journeys. He said to Clive

'I would like to do more sight-seeing jobs, but I don't know how to go about it. How do I get this extra quality work?'

Clive replied 'f*****g hard work.' He knew the amount of effort I put into my business, gaining quality clients prepared to pay decent prices for the upscale standard of professional service provided. We endeavoured to maintain that standard to our hotel.

The six of us, Jean and Clive, Mark and Deanna, and Pam and me, ate together in our Cheam house as well every visit they made, so the friendship was firm. I am not a practical man, but Clive is, being very handy both with design as well as application. That was another reason for them to get on so well, it was another reason why Pam and I jumped at the chance to going into partnership with Mark and Deanna, because they had not only been introduced into our circle of friends, they had been accepted over quite a period of time.

Both Mark and Clive are tall men, each well over six feet, whereas I am only a little fella, I won't say that they looked down on me, but they certainly regarded their stature as superior. I didn't care, because I have always had the confidence to carry off my height, but on reflection this could have been a reason for their ultimate behaviour. As usual, as on most of their trips to the UK, Mark and Deanna met up with Clive and Jean on this visit. We had dinner on the last night before they went to London for their stay before returning to California, and it was during this dinner that it became obvious the two men had already discussed the business relationship. They made it clear that it would have been far more beneficial had those two gone into a business relationship, instead of me and Pam. I wasn't rude, despite their insult, purely because they were so insensitive that they had no idea what they had said.

Clive said to Mark 'it would have been much better if we had got together. I have the money, the practical skills, but I definitely don't have the marketing ability that Harry has. But then again, Jean does.'

It went a little quiet.

Me. 'So you think that matters would be a lot better with you four instead of us four.'

Mark. 'Sorry Harry, but that is definitely the truth. Clive knows his way around a toolbox, and Jean knows her way around a balance sheet.'

Me. 'Ah, but would it even have got off the ground without Pam and me organising everything. You would have just been sitting on your hands, waiting and waiting for the right opportunity. Whereas now, we have a wonderful hotel, prospects as long as they are not harmed by mismanagement, and a great future to anticipate. Unless there's something you're not telling me?'

Mark and Clive exchanged a very meaningful look, which told me so much about the pair of them. Perfidy was in the air. So were secrets.

Mark and Deanna returned back to California, leaving us in something of a state of limbo, but trade was still good, we were gaining an excellent reputation in the hotel trade, and we had successfully kept our expenses manageable.

***

When Mark and Deanna had returned, we again settled into a routine, until I received a phone call from a business lady who was about twenty miles away.

'Hello, is that Mr. Pope.'

'Speaking.'

'Mr name is ..(I honestly can't remember her name, it is not important in any case), 'and I am an interior designer.'

I said nothing, so she continued

'I have been instructed by Mr. _ in America to have a look at the Sheldon Hotel.'

'What for?'

'With a view to re-designing the ground floor of the hotel.'

'It looked OK to me the last time I looked, and that was ten minutes ago.'

'Well, he is the owner, and he has instructed me.'

'Are you aware of the ownership structure of the hotel?'

'He is the owner.'

'Joint owner. In partnership with his wife, me, and my wife. There are four owners. There are four partners.'

'I was not aware of that. However, I have an instruction from him, so I would like to make an appointment to come and view.'

'Let me ask you a question.'

'Yes, what would you like to know.'

'What is your fee?'

'£50 per hour.'

'And how many hours do you anticipate this viewing will take.'

'I like to allow a full day.'

'What, eight hours?'

'That is correct.'

'And who do you expect to pay your account.'

'The hotel.'

'Not the man who has given you the instruction?'

'No, he made it clear that he was not responsible for settling my account, that was the responsibility of the Sheldon.'

'Okay, for the sake of harmony, I will tell you what is going to happen. There is not going to be an open-ended arrangement as to time. You will be here for four hours. No more, no less. I will give you freedom to walk around the hotel, making notes. Before you leave, we will discuss what you have in mind. You will present me with an account, and the hotel will give you a cheque for £200. I will not quibble about your hourly rate. How does that sound to you.'

'Not particularly friendly, and it's not the way that I am used to doing things.'

'Sorry, but that's the way it is. When do you want to come?'

And that was how it was left. The lady made her appointment, and I then sent an e-mail to Mark. I don't have a copy of this e-mail, don't really need one, but it went something like this:

'Morning Mark, have just had an interesting phone conversation with an interior designer lady. I have made an appointment with her for .. and will report back to you. This came right out of the blue, wonder why you didn't think to inform me. Not only rude, but embarrassing.'

The lady turned up on the appointed day and time, suitably dressed. Have you ever noticed how all lady interior designers wear a designer scarf, it's a kind of uniform, and they also often have a letter 'Q' in either of their names. I gave her free access to all public areas, didn't let her loose on any of the guest rooms. She was offered refreshments, which were accepted, and had a lovely wander around. With about half an hour to go, I emerged and sat her down in the lounge so we could have a chat. I also had the company cheque book with me.

'So, what do you think?'

'Well, the hotel owner is my client, so I can't discuss too much with you.'

'Okay, do you want to get paid?'

'Of course.'

'As I explained to you on the phone, there are four partners. Equal. I am one.'

'But he said to me not to discuss with anyone but himself.'

'Okay, then send him your account.'

'We may have an area for compromise. Suppose you ask me questions, then I will answer.'

'What rooms do you think require attention.'

'All rooms on the ground floor.'

'How long will it take for you to complete any contract you may be given.'

'About a month.'

'And how much will these rooms cost? Bear in mind we're only talking about the lounge, bar, dining room, and *possibly* reception.'

'£25,000.'

'What workmen would you use.'

'My own contractors.'

'So you would get a rake-off from them as well as your fee.'

'Putting it crudely like that, yes.'

'I would insist we used my own men who I have used and have complete confidence in.'

'I only use my own staff, and this is non-negotiable.'

'Do you have your account as suggested?'

'Yes, here it is.'

I gave her a cheque for £200.

'Sorry, but you won't be hearing from me again, and I will inform my partner that he won't be instructing you either.'

'I am sorry to hear that. May I ask why.'

'The hotel has only been in our ownership for six months. All money we take is ploughed back, there just isn't anything to spare. Tight budget, and winter's coming, our first winter, and really don't know what to expect.'

'I appreciate that, but bear in mind that if you invest, then you will be able to get a better class of guest, raise your room rates, be better off all round.'

I replied 'yes, I know all that, but we don't have that kind of capital to spare, so we would have to borrow from the bank. I'm not going to go into our finances with you, but due to the property crash over the past three months we are already in negative equity, and the bank just won't lend the money for a project of this nature.'

'Okay, here's my card, I will report back to California in any case.'

'I would appreciate a copy of that report please as the hotel has paid for it.'

Of course, the report never materialised, I never saw a copy of it, I suspect it stayed in American hands, never to be seen again.

I e-mailed my partner after she had gone, along the lines of

'Well, Mark, she's gone, and wanted to spend £25,000 on just the public areas. Do you have that kind of money to spend? I know the hotel doesn't, I know I don't, and I know that I would not be prepared to support any application you may make to the bank if you wanted to raise the money from that direction. What do you think about it all? Can you afford it?'

His reply was along the lines of okay, let's put these plans on hold, but I would want to return to them when the hotel can afford it.

Chapter Nine: Autumn, First Year

We knew that belt tightening was going to be necessary, it was just how it was going to be applied. By this stage as well as Moaner on £25,000, we had two housekeeping staff, two in the kitchen, a Polish man who could put his hand to most things, including night porter, and Pam and me. We worked it out that we were on £2.80 per hour, each, barely sufficient to pay the rent on our flat, so it was a good job that we were eating at the hotel so often. We took nothing else. Mark's attitude by then was that as we were partners, we should take nothing, just like him. His investment equalled our hours in his eyes, so he became increasingly pointed in his comments about the wages we received. The bloke was so dim he couldn't see our point, he never did.

The two in the kitchen were on a combined £25,000, the night porter was living in on minimum wage, the housekeeping were also on minimum. It was becoming increasingly obvious that we couldn't afford Moaner. But I just couldn't bring myself to be ruthless. She had given up her job to come and work for us, I considered it obligatory to remain loyal to her.

Her attitude became increasingly divisive, she wasn't daft, she could see that the hotel had to ditch superfluous staff, and as she was the highest paid with the lowest manual return, it was obvious to all that she was the natural candidate for the chop. However, service had to be continued, we would address that problem when it became really necessary.

That autumn was a difficult period for all of us. Mark was becoming more demanding financially, I stopped sending the money over to California. The accountant was insistent that we didn't send him any more money, because the turnover of the hotel couldn't sustain such a huge hole. We were members of the

Eastbourne Chamber of Commerce, an organisation I have a lot of admiration for. They work for the business community, not just the successful part but also the struggling, as they appreciate their responsibility for the whole.

Every Tuesday I would attend the weekly breakfast meetings, recounting amusing incidents with guests, trying to drum up extra business. One such incident concerned two elderly sisters staying in room eight. This was a twin bedded room.

The ladies were regular guests, staying for a week at a time three or four times a year. They had independent means, lived in the Midlands, always arriving and departing by private taxi. They were absolutely charming, less demanding than some guests, but expecting and receiving individual attention. I always checked that their rooms were spotless, if I wasn't around then Moaner would. It wasn't usually necessary, because the rooms were maintained to an excellent standard by this time.

The sequence of events went like this. The younger sister dropped an earring on the floor, close to the bed, so went on her hands and knees to look for it. Of course, she should have contacted reception, as we would have been pleased to crawl on our knees under the bed. But the sister did instead.

The bed was six inches off the floor, the Hoover would only get so far under, so the middle part under the bed was never accessed. Miss Jane was persistent however in looking for the missing earring, which was worth a not inconsiderable sum as it was made of gold and contained an emerald. She didn't see the missing item of jewellery, but instead discovered something that had obviously been there for quite some time.

It was battery operated, long and thick, smooth one end where the operator had to turn the base, the rest was an uneven, knobbly surface. Twelve inches long, dust had gathered between the distorted section.

In the privacy of their room, the two sisters took it in turns to hold the item, discussing what could be its purpose. They genuinely had no idea, so together bought it to reception, gingerly holding it while they waited their turn in the queue with other guests.

Miss Jane to Moaner, who was behind the desk 'Tell me dear what this is please.'

Moaner 'where did you find it Miss Jane?'

Miss Jane 'under the bed.'

Moaner 'it is obviously lost property, Would you like me to look after it for you?'

Miss Edith 'yes dear, we would, but WHAT is it? We just can't think, and we have no idea. And WHY would it be under the bed?'

I had been in the lounge at the time, popped my head round the door, immediately realised what was occurring. Unfortunately Moaner saw me, and called out 'Mr. Pope, would you kindly come here please and explain to the ladies what this is. They found it under their bed.'

Caught! I could only come forward and examine the item.

'Apologies ladies, obviously it is something that has been left by a previous guest, and missed by our housekeeping staff. You can be assured that they will be spoken with.'

'Yes Mr. Pope, but what IS it?'

Moaner had a big grin on her face, full of expectation.

'May I be adult, and say it's something that should only be used in private. I would feel awkward if you wanted me to say more.'

'Ah, right.' I could hear them both muttering as they walked away to walk up the stairs along the lines of they still didn't understand.

***

Moaner was one of those people who had a really pretty face on a larger than usual frame. She was so pretty, but never had a man friend. Indeed, she engaged at this time without discussion a single lady called Alice. She was stick thin to Moaner's stout. Alice was quite handy to have around, because she would put her hand to a lot of things that others would not.

67

She was in her early twenties, dressed plainly with a short hair style. Average height, I suspected that very few men would seek her company, but she seemed quite happy with Moaner. She was good cover for staff who wanted to take a day off, or maybe ill, and I quite liked her bubbly personality. We didn't pay her very much, as she had a room at the top of the hotel that used to be used by domestic staff when families used to employ such people. We were never full at this time of year, apart from Christmas, so one day when she asked me if she might use the hotel for her address to receive post, I saw no objection. Every few days she would receive padded envelopes with DVDs inside, nothing out of order there.

I had a computer disc with lots of names and addresses of people in the UK, which included over 200 people with the surname of Sheldon. I either e-mailed or wrote to every one, gaining new business this way. I also contacted every single person in the hotel's database going back quite a few years to see if they would like to come for a Christmas package break.

This was for four days, and would be full-on service. All meals were included, two night's entertainment, a mystery coach trip on one afternoon, plus tickets for the Boxing Day pantomime at the Devonshire Park Theatre. We had an excellent take-up, full of bookings by the end of October. Successful marketing.

The Christmas break started on Christmas Eve, and I continued with the tradition of carrying guest cases to their rooms. And they continued with the tradition of not giving a gratuity to the boss.

By 4pm all twenty eight rooms were occupied, and I came down the stairs after the last guest had checked in. Pam was sitting behind the reception desk. I said

'70 – 30'

'What' was her incredulous reply. For once she wasn't on the phone, or chatting to Moaner.

'70 – 30. I hate 70% of our guests, and it's only the first day.'

Of course, Mark was nowhere to be seen when there was work to be done, he was enjoying the break with Deanna in the Californian sunshine. That is why Pam and I were earning £2.80 per hour. Moaner was there, but only just, she soon disappeared leaving everything to be completed by us. Dinner was at 6:30pm, it was my role to take drinks orders as well as serve them pre-dinner. I had a special wine list for the festive break, some extra special lines as well as the usual, with some pretty decent offers. Champagne was of course expensive, especially the Moët, but it was not easy to anticipate the demand. Too much and wouldn't sell until the following spring, too little and the embarrassment of running out during a prime selling period. We must have got it right, at £45 per bottle. I had been watching out for supermarket special offers during November, the optimum time to buy Christmas booze.

After dinner, which finished after a couple of hours, we had entertainment. This comprised a single keyboard player who was pretty good, and he could also sing well. He got the audience going very well, they actually stayed awake until 10:30pm, even buying the occasional drinks. I had taken this eventuality when costing the package.

We managed to get to bed by midnight, all the guests were tucked up, no-one bothered to see in the Christmas day itself. They probably wanted to pace themselves for the physical and demanding activities on offer the next day.

Pam and I arrived at 7:30am on Christmas Day. The night porter said

'The lift isn't working.'

This was the only time in the whole period of our hotel occupation when the thing failed to operate. On the phone to Thyssen Krupp, amazed that they were even there, albeit the phone was diverted to the emergency engineer. He was covering a hell of an area, but promised to be with us as soon as possible, appreciating the predicament we were in. We had a disabled guest on the first floor, in a wheelchair, who couldn't get downstairs for breakfast. Our staff worked wonders, taking his breakfast order, then delivering room service.

Within two hours of our phone call to Thyssen Krupp, the engineer had not only been, but he had fixed the lift. We were back in operation. Splendid service, and from personal experience I can only highly recommend them.

The guest was able to come downstairs for the mid-morning sherry and mince pies. These were home made in our kitchen, delicious, far better than anything Marks and Spencer could provide. Nicely warmed, we didn't offer cream as well, but there was a complimentary brandy to go inside the coffee. Quite a few takers for that, especially with the older ladies.

Lunch was at 1:30pm, we were quite surprised when one elderly couple didn't make it, but we were so busy we didn't think anything more about their absence. That lunch was full on with the service. The booze sold was fantastic, everyone wanted a glass or bottle of wine with their lunch, crackers by every place, party hats, whistles, presents for everyone, we did a pretty good job of looking after them. Two hours later, replete, they disappeared for a snooze either to their rooms, or into the lounge. That was our cue to have lunch, we all sat in the dining room, exhausted, and had our repast. Delicious.

Pam and I dismissed everyone, all the staff went, just us to relax. Then the missing couple arrived.

'Where is our Christmas lunch.'

'Sorry?'

'Where is our lunch?'

'It was served three hours ago. Where were you?'

'In our room, waiting for the call.'

'What call?'

'In every hotel we have previously stayed in for Christmas, they have knocked on our door, saying the Christmas meal will be served in half an hour. We could smell the delicious cooking, so here we are.'

'Did it state anywhere in our Christmas itinerary that we would be knocking on your door?'

'No, but we just assumed.'

'Okay, well, sorry to disappoint, but lunch was three hours ago. If you give us half an hour, we will prepare something for you as best we can. Please go into the lounge and wait'

Aunty Joan, Pam and I went into the kitchen to retrieve what we could, the turkey carcass still had a fair amount of meat on it, there was a lot of stuffing, I got down to it and did some vegetables from the freezer, we turned on the microwave, lucky we still had a packet of Aunt Bessie's frozen roast potatoes, as well as Yorkshire puds, in half an hour we had some fresh gravy, cranberry sauce, and the basics of a reasonable decent meal that wasn't over-cooked, it tasted fresh, the meat was pretty good, and lovely and hot. Really don't know how we managed, but teamwork.

The guests were satisfied, but I didn't give them a free glass of wine. It wasn't my fault they were too thick to work out when to eat.

As I am writing this section, Pam has come into the office. She had a nasty twitch, and quickly disappeared. She didn't want me to see her cry!

We provided a cold plate for dinner at 7pm, quite surprising that everyone turned up, including the missing couple. Excellent appetite. It was just Pam and me for the evening, and while this was being eaten Charles the entertainer arrived.

He had an old piano keyboard with a single speaker. Attached was a microphone so you could hear him singing. At this time he must have been in his early 90s – okay, maybe slightly younger, but that is what he seemed like. He was the only entertainer we could get to come out on Christmas night demanding £150 in cash. He had a dirty old grey suit on, his lank hair was down to his shoulders, with his playing and singing abilities somewhat in question.

His popularity probably reached its heights during WW2. That was when his performance was at its peak, possibly even managing to play every black note and every white note in the correct order. That skill wasn't in evidence that night. He might have known every word when Dame Vera Lynn was also at her peak, but when he played at the Sheldon that night he showed great skill at word and vocal improvisation. Years of practice.

He finished his set right on time at 10:30pm, when he had sufficiently murdered his performance to leave a total of five guests to the end. They were the ones with the hearing aid turned down. But entertainment was all part of the package.

***

Boxing morning arrived with no problems. Lift worked. All staff reported for work on time. All guests arrived for breakfast without complication. Today was pantomime day.

For those readers unaware, pantomime is a British Christmas theatre tradition going back at least 150 years. Men dress as elderly women, young women dress as young men, cast members throw sweets into the audience, children come on stage and play games, everyone screams and shouts, it's all good clean raucous fun. The stars are usually people from television or traditional entertainment, supplemented by local performers.

Eastbourne has quite a few theatres, the Devonshire Park has a traditional pantomime each year written by the director of theatres. I had purchased much earlier on in the year fifty tickets for our guests, but only thirty wanted to go. Miserable lot, all they wanted to do was sit in the lounge, fall asleep, do the crossword, and have some more mid afternoon food. After all, they had paid for it, so they might as well eat it, and tough luck on those who went to the panto. So I was left with twenty tickets to the sell-out afternoon performance. I telephoned BBC Radio Sussex, and was introduced live on air. I told the presenter there were twenty free tickets for families with children waiting at reception, first come first served. Strangely, there wasn't a rush, but all went. They had been budgeted for, and it was the right thing to do.

Pam and I took the night off. That was quite something to do, but we felt we deserved it, leaving the hotel in the hands of Moaner and Alice, as their friendship seemed to be quite a close one. We just needed a break, spending the evening with Aunty Joan, watching telly.

The next day, we waved our guests goodbye.

Tips were something that Pam and I just didn't get involved with, leaving it to the staff to sort out between them. Yes, we received from the guest, but they went into a pot on the kitchen shelf, administered by them, this was quite a dangerous area for us to be involved with and we considered it prudent to distance ourselves. The pot was quite full after all guests had departed.

I gave most of the staff a month off.

We didn't bother to open over the New Year, because very few hotels had much business during this period, not many people wanted to stay, and those that did were either on a budget, or of a rowdy nature and not worth bothering with.

Most of the Polish staff returned to their home country to celebrate the new year, leaving us with Moaner, Alice, and the English housekeeping staff. As there were no guests, we also gave them a break, as Alice could service any rooms we decided to let. Early January business was slow, but steady, with workmen as well as couples, so we knew we had sufficient public interest to keep the hotel open for business. The second week in January Pam and I went away on a marketing trip.

Chapter Ten: January

Part of my marketing strategy was to create a new market. As we had twenty eight bedrooms, all en suite, close to the shops as well as seafront, I knew that our prime position was an excellent selling point. But in our first year, we had only had one coach party stay with us, and I wanted to correct that. I also worked out that a lot of our guests came from East Anglia/Cambridgeshire/Fenland areas, so decided that initially this would be a good area to market.

Before we left, I had a conversation with Moaner.

'I don't feel well,' she said

'I'm sorry, what's the matter?' I was genuinely concerned for her well being.

'I am depressed, and don't know what to do with my life.'

'But I thought you were happy here. The job is easy, the guests are mainly pleasant people, you get on well with the staff, what is there for you to be depressed about?'

'I just don't know where I am going.'

'But we have already discussed this. When we really get on our feet, and make a success of the Sheldon, the plan is to buy another hotel, Pam and I will move into that, leaving you to run this one all on your own. It will be your empire, something to have the complete responsibility, something you have always said that you wanted.'

'Yes, but what if it takes longer than anticipated?'

'What will be will be, dearest Moaner. I can't do any more than I am, you know our plans, you are part of them if you want to be. Your call here.'

There was nothing more I could do or say to her, so we made appointments with quite a few coach companies, two a day where possible, planning on being away for ten days. We left Moaner and

Alice in charge. Staying in cheaper B&B accommodation, it was good to have a little break away from the hotel as well. My older sister lives in Chelmsford, the lower part of the area we intended visiting, so we initially stayed with her for a couple of nights, then moved onto the coach companies. I kept in contact with Moaner, there was a steady small stream of incoming guests, sufficient for us to tick over with limited staff.

We had been away for three or four days, keeping in contact with sister, when she had to be suddenly admitted to hospital for an operation, which proved to be completely successful and no further complications or problems. However, that meant cancelling the marketing plans. I rang the hotel to notify Moaner, but there was no reply. I tried her mobile. No reply. I tried Alice's mobile. No reply. I managed to get through to a friend, who went round to the hotel, finding doors locked, no staff in attendance.

There was nothing for it, I had to leave Pam with my sister, visiting her in hospital to support my brother in law, while I drove the 120 miles back to the hotel. Fortunately no guests were booked in, so all I had to do was open the doors, turn the vacancy sign round, and then start making phone calls. I finally managed to get through to Moaner, no apology, she just informed me that as I was now back she would call in the following day for a chat. Alice was nowhere to be found, it was just me to run the place.

By the next day I had found Alice, who had sheepishly returned. She had told me that she had received permission from Moaner to be absent, on full pay. I told her that she was now back, but she had better behave.

I sat in the dining room with Moaner mid morning, and the conversation went something like this. I am pretty certain of the main accuracy, because it is indelibly seared on my memory.

'What happened the last few days? Are you okay, because you left the hotel closed, unattended, without any authority or permission.'

'I am depressed.'

Believe me when I say that I was patient, understanding, calm, speaking in a caring concerned way to a friend and employee. Nothing aggressive, not patronising, trying to get to the bottom of everything.

'Yes, you mentioned that before, but surely that was no excuse for leaving the hotel in the way you did. Is there something you are not telling me?'

'I hate the hotel. I hate my life, the hotel is making me depressed, I want to give in my notice. The only way that I can continue working here is if I work Monday to Friday only, from nine to five. I can't cope with anything else.'

Now that stopped me talking. I had to think very carefully how to respond. What I wanted to say was 'you stupid cow, we have paid you an exorbitant salary while covering for your shortcomings, tolerated your pathetic behaviour, given you time off when you least deserved it, and still given you a job, when all we wanted to do was get rid of you because you don't deserve to have a position with any degree of responsibility.' But I didn't.

'Sorry to hear that, but of course you appreciate those terms just aren't possible to agree with. We would all like a job like that, but that just isn't going to happen, which I am sure you know already. So do you REALLY want to leave?'

'Yes Harry, I want to leave. Immediately.'

No word of apology for leaving us in the lurch. But then she continued

'I will tell Mark as well.'

Me. 'I didn't know you two were in touch.'

'Oh yes, I have been telling him everything you have been doing with the hotel.'

With that, she stormed off.

Chapter Eleven: What Happened Next

I ran the hotel for the next few days on my own, with the assistance of Alice, while Pam stayed in Essex with my family, and then my brother in law kindly drove her back. I did nothing with Mark for a few days, didn't contact him, left him in the dark. Two people can easily run a 28-bedroom hotel when there are few guests, I cooked breakfasts, Alice housekeeping, we shared reception duties, she went home early and I stayed overnight as porter. But when Pam returned, we had a really long chat about what Moaner had divulged. We decided to do nothing for the present, let him stew for a while. Wait for him to ring me. It took him a couple of weeks before he did, and I just ignored Moaner's bombshell. I wanted to save that one. There was a more pressing matter. Money.

Winter time the hotel lost money, insufficient trade for the overheads, especially the financial commitment to the bank. We needed an overdraft facility, which I discussed with my business manager. He was a really great bloke, appreciated the predicament we were in, especially Mark being cheesed off with me because we hadn't sent him any money at all since November. He must have been hurting, but there simply wasn't enough to send him anything at all.

The bank and I agreed that we needed an overdraft facility of £40,000, but as Mark was not a UK resident Pam and I would have to sign the guarantee. We discussed this with Mark in great detail, explaining that it was necessary for the running of the hotel. He insisted that some money was sent to him in California, I refused, stating that it was an overdraft, not a loan, and only to be used when absolutely necessary. It was not for luxuries, but to keep us afloat, to pay our bills. It wasn't there at the whim of the directors. He really didn't like this, and I had to prove to him all the time when the money was used that it went on hotel bills, not for personal use. That wasn't difficult, because by that stage we were struggling, that forty grand was a lifeline. We didn't arrive at that figure by chance, it was discussed seriously for quite some time, the bank would not let us have a penny more available that was necessary.

But Mark couldn't see it that way, his opinion was still that he should have received a large portion, as he needed it to keep afloat in America. I know that the bank had to speak with him quite a lot, and the business manager came away feeling that he had been talking to a petulant child. Welcome to my world.

We existed those first few winter months, nothing more, this was a period where our friendship with Trish and Dereck became even more firmly embedded. They were there for us, discussed plans, gave advice, moral support.

***

By the very early spring, we needed new members of staff. By this stage we were employing just the Polish couple, their friend as the night porter and general handyman, and one/two housekeepers, depending on how busy we were. Moaner was long gone, the atmosphere considerably improved as it proved she had been a very divisive influence. We took on initially two new members of staff, one male, the other ostensibly female, and as the trade increased another female.

The new male member we ultimately referred to as the traitor, but that was a lot later on, which will be explained towards the end of this book, but as he still lives in the area, I will refer to him in this way from the very beginning. The traitor was a strange man. He was in his early thirties, and could not walk properly. He had a rolling gait, side to side as he propelled himself forward, he was tall, reasonably stout, not scruffy but never really smart. He was quite average really, and his appeal was his versatility.

The traitor was able to run the kitchen on his own, so covered for days off. He ran the bar, not particularly difficult in itself, but handy nonetheless. He answered the phone, covered reception, was computer literate. But what he refused to do was housekeeping, which I found completely understandable. It is a strange lack in the gene of the average man that they struggle to appreciate the finer arts of housekeeping.

Please include me in this deficiency.

During our hotel career that lasted for quite some time this was an area that I had to be constantly trained in. Pam could walk into a room I had thoroughly serviced to my proud satisfaction and find fault in many areas. The Hoover had inexplicably failed to collect all the dust and hairs. There were water stains inside the shower, despite the fact that I had thoroughly wiped, just wearing knickers as it got somewhat wet inside. The bottom sheet on the double bed was insufficiently stretched. The curtains were not folded back in the correct way (I had no idea how I was supposed to learn this most rudimentary basic that was apparent to all women but denied to me). And I had forgotten to replace the toiletries in the shower, as well as making a hash of turning the corners of the toilet roll.

This is an artwork. Do not leave the open end of the toilet roll exposed, that is a sin. It has to be folded into two equal little corners, not over but under, and the toilet roll has to be almost finished before it can be replaced. In all the time we owned hospitality establishments I never once used a toilet roll right from the beginning, we always had a huge store to select from. And the pattern was always the same, because when we went to the larger supermarket or wholesaler we always bought what was the best value on the day, so the toilet roll pattern was always a mystery to me until the almost used latest version found itself in my toilet at home. We would have a surreptitious carrier bag under the cover of darkness full of one quarter toilet rolls, out of date sachets of tomato ketchup, and breakfast cereal packets that had been knocking around for a while, now gone more than a little soft and grateful for the addition of milk to revive them.

So as far as housekeeping was concerned, this was something of a mystery to me, despite years of training. I could see deficiencies in the efforts of others, just like Pam, and could check a room before the arrival of new guests, but the traitor very wisely never ventured into this area. He arrived via an agency when the Polish couple took a two week break, ostensibly because one grandmother had sadly passed away. The traitor proved his worth during this period, so came to work with us. He was initially popular with the other staff, even more so with the guests.

He had a very unfortunate throat complaint, so he had to whisper a lot. That did not impact on his ability to perform his tasks, and we were especially aware, compensating if at all possible. It was very sad really, that he could not speak loudly, but it made you listen all the greater. Pam and I really liked him, we came to rely on him, he was a real asset at the time. But he had one particular physical problem we all had to assist him in overcoming. It was a considerable disadvantage in the kitchen for a chef to be suffering from Crohn's Disease.

For those unaware, it causes inflammation of the digestive system, potentially affecting the lining of the bowel. It is something most unpleasant, even more awkward when preparing food. However, with careful planning and consideration we were able to overcome. He was such a pleasant chap, we considered it very worthwhile to assist in any way we could.

The next new member of staff was Alison. This is not her real name, but sufficiently cloudy to hide her identity. She was a strange one. Stick-thin, she assisted in the kitchen, as well as all other aspects of the running of the hotel, including covering housekeeping when required. I liked Alison, but only at a distance. I certainly didn't want to be her best friend, that was impossible, because she already had one. Her name was Eve.

Alison was in her mid-twenties, one of life's wanderers, not settling down to anything in particular for very long, and we knew that she would be gone by the end of the summer. I can't remember how we found her, and she features on our last day at the hotel as well, so you may care to remember Alison as a character who features at the end of this tale. She had short red hair, which was sometimes dyed different colours. There was a stud in her left nostril, she was clean and presentable, her clothing style could be described as eccentric. Sometimes she would be wearing a skirt, others jeans. She had a very pleasant way of speaking, nothing loud, she considered her words before she opened her mouth. I can't recall her previous career, but I seem to have the memory that she was privately educated. Alison certainly was intelligent, far too good for menial hotel working, but the job suited her at the time, and we were happy to employ her at a basic wage.

After a little while we needed more assistance, and Eve came on board. That was a mistake, because initially we were prepared to overlook her appearance. She had prominent tattoos.

These were up and down her arms, on her neck, and she also had rather unpleasant facial body piercing. We took on Eve because she was the partner of Alison, our judgment was poor here, but in mitigation we did need someone, and it was easier to employ someone recommended than having the bother of interviewing, which had proved problematic in the past.

The employment laws in 2006/7 were just as stringent as they are now, with interviewing techniques limited. As an interviewer, you were not allowed to discriminate because of gender, sexual orientation, potential pregnancy, or any physical blemish. That covered tattoos.

However, we were running a hotel with a clientele mainly over the age of fifty, and Eve's image did not fit ours, so as part of the interviewing I mentioned that she would have to cover her more obvious ink drawings. That did not go down well, but I had to mention how much of a pleasant atmosphere was generated by the staff, and decorum was an integral part. She said she understood, but after a couple of months it became more of an issue, and we had to have a sit down with her. She decided to leave, and a couple of months later Alison went as well.

***

It was during the March of that year, just before Easter, that I lost it with a guest. I don't mean lose my temper, I was uncontrollable with rage, swearing, not caring about the consequences if it resulted in a fight. But it all started so calmly.

To access the car park at the rear of the hotel, you had to drive down a slope under the side rooms that had been added on. No-one had ever bothered to place a restricted height sign to warn drivers. I had never got round to it, believing in the common sense of the guest. I was sitting behind the reception desk when a guest arrived to check in, but had an extremely embarrassed air about him.

He was in his mid-forties, over six feet, slim, looked quite athletic, nice quality clothes, well spoken, with a wife to match.

'I seem to have had a problem getting into your car park.'

'Okay, where is your car now?'

'On the slope before you drive in.'

'Okay, let's go and have a look, shall we?'

I was quite calm, prepared for any eventuality, but I was aghast at what I encountered. The guest had a Volvo estate, with two mountain bikes on the back, connected to a rack. On its own, the car would have had no problem, but because of the extra height of the bikes, the low-ish ceiling was too little for the whole package.

It was jammed.

'May I suggest that you reverse out, so we can have a better look.'

He got behind the wheel with difficulty, as the driver side was very close to the wall. The rear of the estate was the area that was jammed, the bikes on the back connected to the tunnel roof.

He revved up, shot back. Now if he had been sensible, he might have got away with it. His judgment was brute force over subtlety, complete contrast to my driving outlook that is if you are in a potentially problematic situation, do everything slowly and carefully to minimise any possible damage.

However, there was another factor I had forgotten and he was unaware of. There were electricity power lines and telephone wires connected to the roof of the little tunnel. He exited his car, and there was a little group of us examining the result of his lack of driving skills. The wires were broken free, hanging, gently swaying in the spring wind.

The three of us stood there dumbly, him, his wife, and me, only one of us concerned.

He turned round to look at his car, to see his expensive mountain bikes on the rear of the Volvo had buckled wheels. It was his turn to be alarmed.

'Look at my bikes', he exclaimed. 'You'll have to pay for them, no doubt about that.'

No, I didn't lose my temper. I calmly said 'sir, if you had paid attention, then you would have appreciated that the height you were attempting to drive under just wouldn't work with your bikes on the back of your tall estate.' Now I had his attention.

'Now just think for a minute, you have damaged my property by actions, and I think some calm reflection is needed here. Of course, the damage you have caused is your responsibility. We all know that when we do something wrong, we have to be intelligent grown ups. Agreed?'

He nodded, albeit with some reluctance.

'Of course, being a reasonable person, I will mitigate the cost of repair as much as I can. The hotel has a maintenance man, skilled in many areas, repairing the cabling should be well within his capabilities. He was here this morning, so I can ask him to return. He will provide me with a separate bill for this repair. Does that sound reasonable to you?'

By this time he had his hands across his chest. 'Okay, add the cost of repairs to my hotel bill.'

Over the next week I met this guest and his wife quite a few times, always exchanging pleasantries. I had immediately recommended a local cycle repair shop to mend the two bikes, that had been done super fast with the bikes returned by the Monday lunchtime, so their holiday had barely been impacted. My repair man had arrived within an hour on the Saturday afternoon, taken just over an hour to rectify everything, returning cabling and service to normal. I was very satisfied that as an hotelier I had completed everything professionally to the satisfaction of all. That was until it was time to check out.

They were due to leave after breakfast, so I left instructions to be informed after they had paid their account. I was downstairs in my office when I looked up at the tv security screen. I saw them walking down the steps towards the car park, luggage in tow. I was up the back stairs faster than I had ever been before, two at a time which was quite a feat with my little legs.

'Did they pay in full?' I asked Pam.

'Almost.'

'What do you mean, almost?'

'They paid their hotel bill, but not for the damage repair.'

I was off down the central steps, and caught up with them on the pavement outside the hotel.

'Excuse me,' I said in a loud voice. 'You appear to have omitted paying your account in full.'

He looked at me. 'No, I don't think so. I paid for everything I should have done.' He had a stupid superior grin on his face.

Don't forget the age gap, the size difference, and the physical fitness. I was beginning to forget, because I was becoming increasingly annoyed, which in turn gave him more pleasure in his superiority and me increasing frustration.

'What about the damage repair that you did to my hotel. Do you consider £100 unreasonable?'

'No, not at all, considering it was a Saturday afternoon and there was quite a lot to repair, it seemed remarkably fair to me. You obviously have a very competent man there.'

'So why have you not paid this very reasonable £100.' My volume was increasing, which was not very good for Devonshire Place, a select neighbourhood

'Simply because legally I am not liable. I am a solicitor, and have consulted a barrister friend, who informs me that as there was no height restriction notice, there is no obligation on my part. The onus is completely on the hotel to ensure the safety of its guests, which you have manifestly failed to do, so you should consider yourself fortunate that I am not holding you culpable for your negligence. Now, if there is nothing further, I will be on my way.'

I was not just incensed, I was incandescent with rage, no good for my blood pressure, but I was now out of control in my fury.

I shouted 'now look, you cheap chiseller, you might think that you can get away with your fraud at other places, but here in Eastbourne we have ways with dealing with bastards like you. First off, I am parking my car across the entrance so you can't get out. And I am going to check the back of your nasty Volvo estate to make sure you haven't repeated your pathetic error when you arrived. One set of damage is enough for me, thank you very much.'

'I would never stay in a dump like this ever again, my standards are a lot higher, I am used to staying in five star establishments.'

'And I bet you try to walk out without paying there as well. Once a crook, always a crook.'

We now had an audience of half a dozen, local residents attracted by the raised voices, mainly my own. He remained calm throughout, I was increasingly incensed. Pam came out as she could hear raised voices, and came between us, which was more than his wife was doing.

'Come on love, he's not worth getting your blood pressure up. It's obvious that he is not going to honour his word, which obviously counts for nothing, you'll just have to be the bigger man and walk away.'

I looked at the man and his wife, said nothing, took Pam's hand, and with as much dignity as possible walked away and up the steps back into the hotel.

***

The relationship between Mark and myself had broken down considerably by Easter. We were only communicating by e-mails, I had not been rude with him, but found it increasingly problematic having a rational conversation. Pam and I were attempting to run a hotel with our hands tied behind our backs, we had only rented accommodation to live in, all our capital was tied up in the hotel, we could not walk away, we had a business partner who was increasingly irrational in his behaviour and decisions, and a business that was haemorrhaging money at a frightening rate. We really did not know what to do next, and then I received a phone call from a very good friend and fellow hotelier.

'Morning Harry, how are you?'

'Fine, and how's business with you?'

'Just ticking over, we are thinking of buying a different hotel. Had an e-mail from Mark recently, and wonder when it would be convenient to come and look over the Sheldon?'

'You are welcome to come over at any time, friends are welcome for a coffee and social chat, but I wasn't aware of Mark's e-mail. Perhaps you could let me know what it says?'

'Of course, I'll send you a copy, but the bottom line is that he has sent an e-mail to about sixty people, local property agents, other hoteliers, anyone that he thinks might be interested in buying, letting them know it's on the market, but not to bother you as you are busy running the hotel, and to make all enquiries through him.'

My friend kindly sent me a copy of the e-mail, and indeed it showed a list of all recipients. The trouble was, Mark was so naïve, he couldn't appreciate the fact that as the hotel was worth about £300,000 less that we had paid for it just over a year earlier due to the property crash, negative equity meant what it said, and Pam and I would walk away with nothing if the hotel were to be sold. Mark and Deanna would have some equity, but not a lot, the bank would recover their debt, but Pam and I were at the bottom of the pile. There was no incentive for us to sell under those circumstances.

My friend and his wife came round. They were very impressed with what we had achieved, they had a good look at the books, but the complicated ownership situation was sufficient to put them off.

I knew that there had to be another way out, and I saw a possible solution by looking out the hotel front window.

Across the road was an almost identical property. About the same number of rooms, it had previously been a residential home for older people, but had become increasingly unprofitable. The owners had been very receptive when a property development company had suggested it might be converted into flats.

Just a bit of contemporary background may assist here in the narrative. Eastbourne Borough Council has long had a policy of not allowing properties within a couple of blocks away from the seafront to change away from hotel accommodation but allowing change of use for other buildings. The reason is their obsession as a seaside resort destination, maintaining the number of bed spaces throughout the year. However, apart from peak periods, such as 100% occupancy during the summer and Christmas periods, and special events such as the annual air show in August over four days, and the week long tennis tournament in June, hoteliers struggle to fill the bed spaces. That is why Eastbourne traditionally has been such a popular holiday destination for coach companies, which have economy in mind and the guest spend is quite low.

A lot of hotels exist on 60% occupancy rate over the whole year, closing during January and February. Even the coaches don't come during this period, and the theatres are mainly dark. The seafront hotels between the pier and the bottom of Beachy Head were built during the Victorian period and have had to be adapted for luxurious necessities such as electricity (late 1880s), bathrooms (undated) and access for the disabled.

The Victorian builders had no regard for the handicapped in wheelchairs for example, and the front access usually has many steps. Ramps are impractical, as the slope would usually be too great, which of course was the case with the Sheldon. The rooms of most hotels are rarely converted for handicapped occupation, if the seafront hotel had say 80 rooms, only two or three at best would be suitable. The financial costs of conversion would far outweigh the room rate. Eastbourne Borough Council's stance could be understood from the viewpoint of the physically handicapped, but not from the practical day to day running of a hotel that had to be economic.

However, the Council's rigid policy of not allowing any hotel change of use became diluted the further away from the seafront. The Sheldon was one block back.

I drew up a ten page planning document, showing how the Sheldon could be converted into flats.

The first hurdle was to prove that the hotel was uneconomic. I had to show in the books as an addendum that it was impossible to make any money running the building as a hotel, because the Council would not look at any project that failed to jump over this first hurdle. To aid, I obtained confirming documents both from Bank and Accountant, as they were well aware of what was happening between Mark and me, and especially the Bank wanted to cover their position. They were pretty exposed by this time, and my friendly relationship with the senior business manager was still very amicable, because I had him on side and aware of all and any ideas I may come up with.

The project director of the conversion was, of course, most helpful. To make it work, we had to calculate the cost of the whole project from start of planning to start of conversion. I had an uphill task in convincing the following:

- *My business partner*
- *Eastbourne Borough Council planning department*
- *The bank to fund yet another speculation*
- *An investor to underwrite and then join in the profits*
- *A builder with sufficient experience and savvy to see a project like this from start to finish.*

***

To be successful, I had to have Mark on board right from the word go, because his obduracy had become impossible. I sent him a detailed e-mail, planning the project point by point that even he could comprehend. It also channelled my thoughts, so I could concentrate on making it work, ignoring fringe ideas. The bigger picture was fine, but the main plan had to work first.

The main selling point for both Mark and me was that we could walk away with a potential profit from a project that had been a financial disaster from the start. It was going to take at least a year just to plan, let alone convert into flats, which would be the easy part. The hotel was worth two thirds what we had paid for it, we were only repaying interest, very little capital had been reduced, the insecurity had been the sole factor in reducing our relationship to zero. With both of us behind it, we stood a chance of success.

The trouble was, he was basically thick, and because it was me behind the idea, Mark was less than enthusiastic. He wanted to either sell the hotel at a loss, or run it until it regained its capital value. No third option, and as the first would not work for either of us, there was only number two, with him unable to do anything from thousands of miles away. He was understandably frustrated, but I was not being helpful either because he couldn't make his mind up. I went ahead with the planning in any case, because I saw so much merit in it that even Mark might come round in the end.

I had a couple of informal talks with council officials, who I had previously had an excellent relationship with. If approached in the right way, they were not unreasonable people, and I knew how to play their game. You communicate frankly with a plan, and ask their opinion in principle if it would work. The impression I gained was there was just a possibility that if planning was prepared properly, financial charts showing lack of viability, extra residential accommodation provided in an area that would benefit, then it might be favourably considered.

The biggest stumbling block was finance. The project's viability had to be proven in advance, with the bank's exposure of £600,000 plus £40,000 overdraft against a property worth just that taking priority over all other guarantees. £50k had to be allowed for planning, stumbling blocks to be overcome, and then there was the project itself. Twenty flats at an overall average of £150k each equals £3m. Take away £700k, and there was £2.3m before conversion costs and underwriting finance. Not a great deal of profit margin, certainly not as close as other projects the builders had planned, with a lot more complications. Someone had to underwrite the planning £50k costs, the bank made it very clear they would not, the builders would not as they were permanently underfunded, so the whole project was doomed from the start over the lack of investment.

Barry the project director did tell me an amusing tale when we were chatting at length about my ideas. They had purchased the building opposite the Sheldon from the owners of the nursing home with full planning permission, but had completely overlooked a local inconsistency.

Eastbourne is a strange town, only developed after the arrival of the railways in 1849. The land had been owned by the Duke of Devonshire mainly to the west of the pier and up to the bottom of the promontory Beachy Head. Most of the land to the east of the pier was owned by a prominent land owning family, so when building commenced freehold ownership of property was conveyed on the agreement of local building covenants. You were not allowed to alter your property without the permission of Devonshire Estates, or change the use. The seafront hotels are especially restricted, with buildings only painted certain subtle colours. No commercial properties are allowed on the seafront except for hotels, so no amusement arcades, no restaurants, and no pubs.

Permission is usually granted as a formality unless the plan is outlandish, and three weeks before the sale was due to go through the solicitors acting for the nursing home had to go to Devonshire Estates cap-in-hand to ask for permission. After making them wait, this was granted, but only after a fee of £25,000 had been paid. I asked the inevitable question

'How much would it have been if not under any pressure.'

The answer from Barry was '£5,000'.

So, for the sake of some common sense and an investor who was willing to underwrite the project we were still stumped, stuck in a business partnership that none of us wanted

***

It was at this stage I had a visit from a very unexpected guest. You may recall that I had a clause inserted in the contract when we purchased the Sheldon to prevent the previous owners from owning a hotel within a ten mile radius and two years of the date of purchase. David came calling, asking if he may be excused from this restriction. We have always had a decent relationship, no animosity for any reason, so I asked him which hotel he was thinking of buying. It was the closest one to the Sheldon, within fifty yards.

Ask yourself, what would you do?

'Would there be any competition between us?' I asked.

'No, don't think so. It is a completely different customer base to the Sheldon, coaches, evening entertainment, packages.'

'Whatever makes you want to return to the hotel trade? It's only 15 months since you left it. Are you bored?'

'Yup, I am too young to retire, I do enjoy what I do.'

'That's okay with me, then, if that is what you want, go ahead and buy. I'll have a word with my solicitor so there's no legal problems, but best of luck to you.'

We shook hands, he bought his new establishment, it was never a problem to either of us. There was absolutely no point in being unreasonable, I saw no area of potential conflict, and it transpired that we never had to have any kind of disagreement. To the contrary, on more than one occasion we would help each other if one hotel was full.

Chapter Twelve: Interesting Guests

I am going to pause here with some recollections of amusing incidents with guests. I know I have mentioned some already, but more will bear telling. The first concerns Beachy Head.

This is a couple of miles to the west of the town, a series of chalk cliffs well over six hundred feet high. There is constant erosion, as the Environment Agency has a policy of allowing wearing away to occur naturally. It is a beauty spot, lots of tourists visit, especially non-English student parties, the disused coastal lighthouse has been converted into an upscale bed and breakfast.

Anything up to fifty poor souls commit suicide from the Beachy Head cliffs every year, despite the best efforts of the Chaplaincy Team. These volunteers patrol every single day of the year, a dedicated team who give their time willingly.

However, it does sometimes happen that guests disappear from their bedrooms, leaving possessions mysteriously behind. Then it becomes the responsibility of the accommodation provider to report the disappearance to the appropriate authorities.

On this occasion, the first clue that we had was when she didn't come down for breakfast. You have to be vigilant as a hotelier, ensuring that only guests enter the premises, and if they have not paid for their meals for some reason, then don't let them have a free breakfast. However, the vast majority ate with us, especially breakfast. The lady had not stayed with us previously, booked in for five nights, failed to materialise for breakfast morning of day four.

Housekeeping have a computerised check list for each room, so they know if it requires more attention for the next occupant. They tidy up the possessions, Hoover, make sure that nothing unsociable has occurred in the room, clean the shower, empty bins, replenish the refreshment tray. However, this lady's bed had not been slept in, no sign of occupancy since the previous day.

She was a single lady, late 40s, a London address, nothing memorable about her appearance, hadn't spoken much to any of us since Moaner had checked her in, so there wasn't a lot of information to share about her. Of course, she had the key ring with front door and room, which was missing with the absent guest.

We discussed between ourselves, but did nothing until the morning of day five, when she was due to check out. The account had been paid in full, so there was nothing to alarm us apart from her absence. Housekeeping packed her belongings very carefully into her one case, all was kept secure in our office, so we rang her mobile number. It went to voice mail.

In those days it was far more common to use *Ask Jeeves* as a search engine rather than Google, so I entered her details. Nothing materialised. We had a very good relationship with the local police, we had the phone number of the community officer, so I had a discreet word with him, just in case she had decided to have a one way trip to Beachy Head.

The next day on the local news it was announced that a female body had been found at the base of the cliffs, description not that dissimilar to our missing guest. I contacted my local policeman, no, he said, she is not your guest, might be close description, but not close enough. Keep the case open, see what happens.

Two days later she came into reception as if nothing untoward had happened.

'Do you have my case please.'

'Certainly, Harry will just get it for you.' Pam paused, after sending me downstairs.

'We were a little worried about you, wondering where you were. It is a little unusual to lose a guest for a few days.'

She leant into the desk so she could speak quietly to Pam.

'I must confess that I have been having a very naughty time. You see, I have a very good job, and wanted to have a very quiet break for a few days. My position is very high pressure, so I just *need* some time for myself. I had dinner in an excellent local Italian restaurant on my own. I left quite late, just as one of the staff was also leaving, he asked me if I would like to join him as he was going to have a drink. It transpired that he had a few days holiday owing, so one thing led to another, and I have spent the last three days in bed. He gave me the best sex I have ever had in my life, I am still glowing all over, I know we will never meet again, but that doesn't matter. It was also the best holiday of my life, so thank you for the stay, it has been great, but I think you will understand why you won't be having me as a guest again.'

Pam had a look on her face when she replied that had understanding written all over it.

'Ah, here's Harry with your case. So pleased your stay has been an enjoyable one, really glad that you are a satisfied guest.'

***

I have been a writer for many years, not much success until recently because I haven't put sufficient effort into it. Shortly after arriving in Eastbourne in the summer of 2003 I joined a writers' circle, becoming chairman for two years. By the time we owned the Sheldon, the circle was meeting monthly on our premises for free. The financial state of the club wasn't too healthy, membership static, it was the ideal solution.

A few weeks previously, there had been a launch of the summer and pantomimes coming that year at the Devonshire Park Theatre. The invitation was for hoteliers and anyone of influence who could potentially publicise the two shows. The pantomime was to star Sue Holderness, Marlene from *Only Fools and Horses*, the summer show was By Jeeves, with Jeffrey Holland in the starring role. Jeff had starred in various comedy television shows, such as *Hi De Hi, You Rang My Lord,* and *Oh, Doctor Beeching!*

I got into conversation with Jeff, asking him where he was staying during the three week run.

'A pal of mine has a flat close to the theatre, but I have five days where I have no-where to stay.'

He was such a pleasant man, very easy to chat to bearing in mind his show business success.

'How about staying at the Sheldon. I will give you a double room for the price of a single, so your wife can come and stay if she wants to as well.'

'That's very kind Harry, I will take you up on your offer.'

When staying, Jeff was at a loose end on the Tuesday night, which was to be the meeting of the writers' circle. Not only that, we held an annual short story competition of maximum 1,000 words, which as chairman I was due to read out. We were in the bar, chatting after dinner.

'If you are not doing anything this evening, fancy sitting in on our writing meeting? It's the short story competition.'

'Tell you what,' said Jeff, 'if there aren't too many entries, I will read them out for you.'

He was as good as his word, and there is really something, hearing your words being read out by a professional actor, one who knows what he is doing, not like some of the amateurs who make out they do. We had a dozen entries that year, next year we invited him and his wife Judy Buxton to come and stay as well as read out. That was the start of our friendship, we are still good mates all these years later.

We invited Jeff to become a patron of the club, a role he relished for quite a few years, giving his time without hesitation, also professional opinion when members asked him to read their work.

A couple of years ago we joined Jeff and Judy who were on a Cruise Maritime voyage on the Marco Polo. It was a *Comedy Legends* theme, so we were able to socialise with them over a memorable twelve nights.

***

Bear in mind that at the start of our ownership, all bookings were entered into a diary by hand. Nothing on computer, we had to instigate that system from scratch. It was the very start of the *Booking.com* revolution, we didn't ever install their system, Trip Advisor was in its infancy, so we took bookings on the phone, off the street, or by e-mail. Sometimes you could come unstuck.

Moaner was on the reception desk when she had a couple ask for a double room. They seemed okay, paid cash for two nights Sunday and Monday, but more and more people were coming through the front door without previously booking. The initial couple were in their mid thirties, he was just under six feet, athletic, slim, she was dark haired, lined face, dressed nothing out of the ordinary.

The next lot were a couple with three children, quite similar, looked like they could be related to the first couple. Our very large family room on the first floor was available, which had a double bed and also a single in the corner. Moaner gave them this room. By the time that the late afternoon arrived, Moaner was gone, I was behind the reception desk. I asked the extra people what room they were in, to be told the same room that the first couple had booked. I went upstairs behind them, when they entered the room, I asked to come in as well. They didn't have a lot of option but to comply, and I discovered four adults and three young children with lots of luggage scattered everywhere. The room was already a mess.

'This room has a maximum occupancy of three people. That is a double bed, that is a single. No room for three children.'

'That's okay sir, the kiddies can sleep with us.' This was stated in a broad Irish accent. It was obvious to me that they were part of the travelling community

'No, that will not happen. If you want to have all of you stay, then you will have to book another room, and pay for it.'

'But we can't afford another room.'

'I want to be reasonable and helpful here, but look at it from my point of view. I am running a hotel on a very tight budget, need all the occupancy I can get, it's no good if I allow you to have so many in one room. I have another family room, you can have that at the same rate as this one. How does that sound.'

'Okay guvnor, here's the cash.' They peeled off the money, I went downstairs for the other room key. I thought that was it, but I was sadly wrong.

I was still behind the reception desk when the two couples came downstairs and went to walk out the front door.

'Excuse me', I said in a loud voice, 'where are the children?'

'They are asleep in the bedroom.'

'You're not going to leave them while you go out.'

'We won't be long, we're just going for a bite to eat.'

I put my firm voice on. 'We are not taking responsibility for your youngsters. If you walk out that door, then I am ringing Social Services. I don't want to do this, but you are leaving me no choice.'

The dark haired mother walked up to me in a very threatening manner. 'You do that and we'll torch the place.'

I turned round and shouted into the kitchen 'in here now, I've got a problem.'

Pam rushed out, with Anya, Artur and Baby Artur behind. I took money out of my pocket, and said 'we don't respond to threats. I want you out and off my premises. I am ringing the police so they are aware of what's occurring, here's your money back, upstairs and pack. And when you leave, I want my keys back as well.'

I am not a brave man, only a little fellow, but there was no way that I was going to back down. Fortunately for me, they did, leaving with very intimidating looks. I knew there was going to be trouble later. The police were informed, there was nothing they could do, other than promise to have a patrol come pass every now and again if they had nothing else on.

Pam went home that night on her own, I bedded down in the lounge so I could keep an eye on everything during the night.

The night porter went to bed in the basement. The lounge lights remained on throughout the night.

Some time around one am, I was just dropping off in the uncomfortable window seat, when there was a loud noise of a car revving its engine outside the hotel. Then the car horn sounded, insistently discordant at the silent hour. People were turning their lights on in adjoining buildings, I was looking out the window, when all four car windows came down. Of course it was the noisy ex-guests, what could I do but stare out the window. After a minute, I realised that this was making them continue, aggravating their already sense of disrespect. I came away from the window, not to be seen. They got bored after a while, and with a final long blast on the horn they were away. We never saw them again, but I didn't nod off again that night.

Chapter Thirteen: More Bombshells

We stumbled through that summer, facing everything with equanimity. Staff were talking to each other, guests were checking in, the hotel was making a profit, Mark and me were writing e-mails to each other, the accountant was independently verifying everything I was doing to Mark so he was satisfied as to the probity, we were paying our bills, and the weather was a good summer.

The traitor's reliability was becoming suspect. He was taking more and more time off due to his Crohn's Disease, we understood completely and supported him throughout, but then the staff refused to work with him, and I had to have a private chat with him which was very unpleasant for me.

We had always adopted a rigid tip policy. I never received any, not once, despite exerting and blowing hard when carrying cases to rooms, and when guests settled their account on departure and added something for the staff, we placed all cash in a box in the kitchen, so they could share it out between themselves. We were only the conduit, it was a dangerous area for a hotel owner, I wanted nothing to do with the tip money. I was quite sure that the housekeeping staff would pocket anything left in the rooms for themselves, not sharing, but if they did, then that was up to them. But about £140 went missing from the tip box in the kitchen, kept hidden away in a drawer, and his colleagues pointed the finger at the traitor. Now I had to reluctantly become involved.

Pam did not want to be involved in our conversation, so I sat down with the traitor.

'You are aware that the missing £140 hasn't been found.'

'Yes Harry, and I have no idea where it is.'

'You are also aware that your colleagues refuse to work with you in the hotel.'

'Yes Harry, and I can't understand why. I didn't take it; it wasn't me, but I can't convince them otherwise.'

'I have been placed in an impossible situation. The smooth running of the hotel has been jeopardised, the worst possible accusation has been made against you, and despite the fact that there isn't a shred of evidence who took it, I am being backed into a situation where I am going to lose a friend, as well as a key member of staff. Help me out here, what do you think is a possible solution.'

'Harry, I love working here, with you and Pam, but I don't want to lose my job. I need the money, I love the hotel work, I don't know what I would do. I don't know what the solution is.'

'Well, you can front it out. Maybe in time the others will come round, but I have seen this situation before in a workplace, and it always ends up the same way – they go. Also, bear in mind that we will be cutting back staff in a couple of months' time, when autumn/winter business slows down, and you are the one most likely to go. I am trying to be fair here, but also realistic. I don't happen to think that you did it – it just isn't in your personality – but that's not what the others think, and them ousting you is what they want.'

'So you won't support me, then.'

'I will sit on the fence. I have always made my situation clear, Pam and I don't get involved with the tip money. If the staff can't sort it out between themselves, then we will refuse it every time. If you can't sort out this mess, then it's time for you to consider your position.'

By the end of the week he was gone.

Alison had already gone by this stage. And so had Eve. I had tried tactfully to point out that her tattoos and piercings just were not compatible with the type of hotel we were trying to run, but she just could not see it. Her attitude was 'if they don't like it, then they shouldn't look'.

My unreasonable attitude was 'cover them up so they are not in the guests' faces'. The parting of the ways was inevitable. I was quite sad in a way, because although I appreciated the fact that Eve was a very good worker, she had allowed her hobby to overcome her ability to pursue her chosen career. She was a very intelligent young lady, and I am quite sure she has found her niche in life.

Alison was completely different. She was sly, had come recommended by Moaner, and I never gave her the responsibility she desired. There was conflict between her and the traitor, and she only lasted less than six months in the hotel. I always felt that there was something underlying in her makeup, a sentiment that Pam didn't share. She thought that Alison was genuine, a good worker, and one to be valued.

***

That summer was a period of calm before the storm. We had no idea what the future held, only insecurity, so it was with a great sense of surprise that we answered the reception bell while breakfast was being served during the second week of September.

This was traditionally a time when we were very busy, because children had returned to school, and the retired generation wanted to come to Eastbourne for their breaks. We could easily have close to 100% occupancy during this period, going into October, because the guests were not rigid with their dates. If we were full, then all they did was arrange to stay when we had vacancies. This particular week was not full, so we were able to accommodate our unexpected guests.

Mark's wife Deanna was a very quiet woman, a very pleasant person who had found wealth initially a surprise, but soon overcoming when she was able to indulge in lots of whims, often connected with the shopping channels. She had an older sister who looked like a Barbie doll, very slim figure, chic blonde hair from a bottle and a pony tail, happy to spend her sister's money on expensive designer clothes so she could attract younger men. At the time she was married to a male model type who was at least ten years her junior, and of course to keep the relationship fresh she was very happy to spend money on her wardrobe as well as appearance. She didn't work.

Their mother was a really lovely lady. She worked in the factory in California with Mark and her husband, investing their savings in his business many years previously. They were simple folk, unused to the trappings of wealth, dressing simply, eating unhealthily, very satisfied with their lots so they could allow their son in law full independence with their investment.

The surprise guests that September morning were Deanna's mother and sister.

Pam and I were completely taken aback by their arrival, complete with luggage. I asked

'When did you arrive?'

'We have just flown in.'

'How long are you planning on staying?'

'Just for a few days.'

'Where are you planning on staying?'

'Why here of course,' said in such a manner that I was an idiot for even thinking otherwise.

'But this is a peak season for us. You had better come into the lounge so we can continue this conversation more privately.'

The four of us walked into the lounge, sat down, and I asked

'Now, why are you here?'

'We wanted to have a look at the hotel, see how it is going.'

'What you really mean is that Mark doesn't trust me, and wanted you to come over to spy.'

'No need to be aggressive.'

'Okay, how would you take this situation if it was you? Calmly? I haven't heard anything from the man for weeks, and then you arrive on my doorstep expecting immediate accommodation, I assume for free. I am not being unreasonable, please note that I am speaking in a calm and rational way while trying not to give any form of offence, which of course has been created by your unannounced arrival. Of course, as Deanna's family, you are welcome here at any time as honoured guests, everything provided courtesy of the hotel, but that is proving difficult bearing in mind the circumstances.'

'Don't worry Harry, we are only here for three days, we just want to check that all is going well and report back to Mark and Deanna.'

'May I ask? Have you made any appointments to see the Bank?' I paused. 'The Accountant?' Another pause. 'The solicitor?'

I gave them time to consider these questions.

'Would you like me to make appointments for you? What I will do is, give you time today to recover after your long flight, and then make these appointments tomorrow and the day after. I will escort you round to the office, introduce you, and then leave you there. I do not wish to be present while you discuss business. I don't feel it is my place to listen in while you ask lots of questions and receive unpalatable answers.'

They both nodded their heads.

'Now, you are very lucky, One of our executive rooms is free, so give me an hour to arrange with housekeeping so it is ready for you, and we will book it out. I will organise some refreshments in the meantime, so if you would like to stay here in the lounge coffee and pastries will be on their way. Your luggage will be waiting for you in your twin bedded room.'

Over the next hour or so I arranged all I had said I would, so they had their three appointments. We did not offer to socialise with them, Pam and I just didn't feel like making small talk with people come to examine minutely how we were running their family investment. They looked at us as employees in any case, we were not to be trusted and they wanted to eat at times that didn't necessarily suit us. The pair of them disappeared during the day, retiring to bed very early, so we saw them next at breakfast.

I escorted them round to the solicitor's office, and introduced them to the man who was more of a friend to Mark then me, as he saw the balance of power in that direction. I left them there after ensuring that they knew the way back.

That afternoon was the turn of the accountant, with the same procedure. The next morning completed the sessions with the bank, who were particularly keen to meet Mark's representatives so they could have a better idea as to plans. I knew full well that the two ladies had no independent opinions, they were there purely to find out a one sided viewpoint. They returned by late afternoon, so Pam and I sat down with them in the lounge for a clear the air chat.

'Well ladies, have the last couple of days been revealing to you?'

'They certainly have.'

'Now do you feel better disposed towards Pam and me?'

'Slightly so. We can now appreciate the pressures you have been working under, and it was especially revealing talking to the accountant. He was very forthcoming, and it's his advice we will be taking back to Mark.'

'And what is that advice.'

'That he keeps the hotel.'

'Fine, so where does that leave Pam and me?'

'I don't understand.'

'Well, at present, he wants to retain his share of the hotel. He always seems to forget that we are partners, not employees, so what he decides doesn't necessarily go. Maybe Mark would like to buy us out instead.'

'But Mark doesn't have any spare cash at present.'

'That is blindingly obvious. When he does manage to get his finances in order, then he may very well then decide that he doesn't want the hotel after all, and place his share on the market.'

'That is for Mark to decide, we can only return with our impressions.'

'So we are to be left in limbo, an uncertain future still, at the whim of a man who doesn't trust us.'

'If that's how you choose to see the situation.'

'Okay ladies, Pam and I will act accordingly. When are you away?'

'We are being collected at nine tomorrow morning.'

***

The next morning they had their usual breakfast, and we were sitting in the lounge window waiting for their lift. That is when the next surprise occurred.

Their lift was Clive and Jean.

They seemed completely unconcerned at being there, unembarrassed that they hadn't bothered to be in touch for quite a few months, and that here they were, our supposedly very good long-standing friends, on the side of the people who wanted to undermine our lives. Pam and I were flabbergasted at their perfidy. What disappointed us the most was the way they treated long-standing friends without care for our feelings. One phone call the previous day would have gone a long way to alleviate our sense of being let down by people who we had known for so many years, through a lot of bad times as well as good, and who we had introduced to Mark and Deanna.

Anyway, there was nothing to be done, all we could do was be polite, civilised, offer hospitality, and then see the party on their way, but the relationship could never be the same again.

***

Pam and I had a decision to be made. Did we stay on as employees and directors of the hotel, never knowing how long it was going to last, or did we decide to walk away. We had a long chat with auntie Joan, whose opinion was very relevant because any decision would impact on her life as well. By this time she was 90, still very fit and active, but reliant on us for her well being and living accommodation. I have no idea if we made the right decision, but we resigned as directors and employees, giving two months' notice that we would be leaving the hotel.

We did this through the solicitor, simply because he was looking after the interests of the hotel, communicating with both parties, and any legalities and consequences would have to be carefully weighed. We thought that two months was sufficient time for the legalities to be completed, even at the slow pace of the UK legal system.

1st November was to be our first day free of the hotel.

We were fair to our staff, letting them know what was occurring. Yarik, who had been with us since the start of the year, made it clear that the day we left was the day he would depart as well. I tried to persuade him otherwise, but he was determined to return home to Poland, as he felt that his time had come to go back. The two housekeepers didn't want to change, who could blame them, so they decided to take their chances with Mark.

We made as many arrangements as we could, anticipating where we would live, and what we would do for a living. We were walking away with nothing.

On the 31st October, 10am, the accountant arrived for the changeover. He was accompanied by Moaner, who was to be general manager on behalf of Mark. She was not to have hands on however, that role was to be performed by none other than Alice, who had been in touch with Moaner all the time, watching and waiting.

I was polite, and said to the two women 'do you have a licence to serve alcohol?

'No,' was the reply, 'we are taking the exam in a few weeks' time.'

'Then I will not allow my personal licence to be used on the hotel's behalf, and require the bar to be locked and no booze to be sold at any time.' I looked at the accountant. 'I expect you to ensure that this is enforced,' as I handed him the bar keys.

And that was it. We walked away from the hotel.

Chapter Fourteen: Explanations

What happened afterwards?

Alice was the manager for quite some time, and we understood that she converted one of the premier downstairs rooms into her own accommodation. She painted the walls a dark purple, with strange symbols, and in the middle of the room from floor to ceiling she had an extra built in as a special feature. A pole so she could practice her hobby and maybe have an alternative career.

Moaner decided that she wanted to continue being in charge, a role she performed with great aplomb until she was peremptorily dismissed by Mark as she was costing him too much with very little signs of actually doing anything. She found herself a boyfriend, lived on a boat, and got a menial job in the local hospital. It has been a great surprise to me not to have seen her when visiting as a patient.

Yarik went back to Poland, where he got married, and now lives on a farm with his extended family.

Anya and Artur still live in the area, Pam and I still see them occasionally, we get on very well with them because we always treated them with respect. They are a lovely couple, still together after all these years.

Trish and Dereck are still our best friends.

What happened to Mark and Deanna? The saddest part of all this sorry story is she contracted cancer, and passed away after a short battle. I subsequently understood that they had initially purchased their share of the hotel so he may have an English business interest after her passing, especially as they both loved the UK so much. She was a lovely lady, completely under his influence when it came to business, and in thrall of his ability to provide the funds to underwrite her spending.

I do not know for certain what occurred to Mark, but can only surmise. I know that his financial problems worsened, and it must have been a very difficult period for him. His problem with me was lack of communication. I have had many years to reflect, and have come to the conclusion that had he bothered to be open and honest with me at all stages, then we would have been able to work round the financial difficulties. However, he regarded me as an employee, not partner, so didn't bother to share relevancies. He may have sold his Californian car part business, and I have researched it online with no mention of him being involved. His published e-mail address is still active and relevant to his former business but this may be an internet anomaly.

That doesn't mean to say that he is not still interested, but he now lives some hundreds of miles further south, towards the Mexican border, in a desert community.

The subsequent story of Pam and me is not so straightforward. We had a period of reflection after departing the hotel, but finances took us over. The bank contacted us for payment of the £40,000 overdraft, as we had stood guarantee. Mark denied any knowledge of this huge sum, said it was all down to me, he hadn't signed anything, he hadn't gained any benefit, he had paid out enough already and refused to admit any degree of responsibility. Pam and I had already maxed out our credit cards on the hotel's behalf, to a further £30,000, and we were right up the creek without any way of creating a forward motion against the tide. What we found particularly galling was the fact that we had paid out all that money over the hotel ownership, sunk literally everything we had into it, committed our futures, and were left holding the baby while he was nursing his financial wounds back home. He certainly didn't get off without losing a great deal of dollars.

The following Spring, we went bankrupt.

At the time it cost us £495 each, money we didn't have, so had to be subbed by Aunty Joan, who continues to live with us.

The bankruptcy court even took my three original ERNIE savings bonds from the first 1955 draw, which I had held onto for all those years. I did everything right, declared all known assets as well as debts, and for the next two years struggled emotionally with the shock of losing everything. And then something wonderful happened. I looked in the cupboard under the stairs, and realised that I still had my late father's collection of vintage comics. They were to be the financial basis for me buying and selling unusual items. I would attend auctions, then sell on a Sunday morning at boot fairs. I never made a lot out of it, but it was sufficient for us to keep our heads above water until we worked out what we wanted to do.

I am now a funeral celebrant, taking non-denominational services. And I am also a public speaker, on a variety of topics. So all's well that ends well. It is now early 2019, Pam and I have just celebrated our 45th wedding anniversary.

My publisher, Joe at Andrews UK, is very pleased with me. My first book in the 'Secrets' series, Buried Secrets, is selling very nicely, so he wants another to complete a trilogy. This will be called 'Chauffeur Secrets', and the first few pages follow as a taster.

What Happened to the Hotel?

Mark continued with his ownership, with Moaner in charge, and Alice responsible for the day to day running. However, he knew that he was on a financial loser, continuously trying to negotiate with the bank. The accountant was a great help to him during this period, realistic advice that was mainly ignored. However, the bank were pulling all the financial strings, they had the greatest potential fiscal disaster. By this time the mortgage commitment was just over £600,000, the hotel was worth in the region of £50,000 more. Any potential buyer would have to re-vamp, with books that were hardly healthy, and a management structure sufficient to put off most buyers.

The bank ultimately had no alternative but to foreclose.

It was placed on the market, we were kept aware of developments through insisting that we were still in the loop. It was quite an effort, rumours abounded, various people were allegedly interested, but in reality no firm offers were made.

An empty hotel with no trade with the bank as the seller meant it went for peanuts of £500,000, just about half we paid less than three years earlier. Mark and Deanna took the greatest financial hit of course, the new businessman buyer had quite a project on his hands.

I won't go into too much financial detail here, it's not my place to do so, but what has occurred is some of the rooms were converted into larger executive ones, walls removed, and instead of a 28 bedroom hotel, he was left with one of twenty. The hotel went so cheaply, it was possible to invest. The new owner however had other business interests in Europe, so he decided to lease it out, which is now the case.

The couple who are now running the hotel are really good at it. They do everything they can to increase trade, no evening meals any more and it's called a bed and breakfast, no hotel in the name. They are doing everything right, and deserve all success that hopefully comes their way.

If you enjoyed this book, you might also like...

Lightning Source UK Ltd.
Milton Keynes UK
UKHW041417030719
345496UK00001B/1/P